Veteran Recall
Americans in France Remember the War

Hilary Kaiser

with a preface by Brigadier general
James S. Dickey

HEIMDAL

Layout design and interior design by Erik Groult
Cover design and production by Philippe Gazagne

Layout by Nord Compo
Copy editor and editorial production by Gabrielle Baqué

ISBN 2-84048-194-4
All photographs, postcards, and documents have been generously
loaned by the people mentioned in this book.

Editions Heimdal
Château de Damigny – BP 61350 – 14406 Bayeux cedex
Tél. : 02.31.51.68.68 – Fax : 02.31.51.68.60 – E-mail : editions.heimdal@wanadoo.fr

For My Three Sons

The next thing most like living one's life over again seems to be a recollection of that life, and to make that recollection as durable as possible by putting it down in writing.

Autobiography, Benjamin Franklin

PREFACE

We owe our World War II veterans a huge debt – a debt of honor. As partial payment of that debt, in June 2004, we are celebrating those veterans at the 60th anniversary of D-Day, and next year will see the 60th anniversary of the World War II victory celebrations. Sixty years. ...

A little perspective is in order. In 1925, we celebrated the 60th anniversary of the end of the American Civil War. For those Americans who grew up in the early years of television, no memory is more poignant than the regular countdown of America's Civil War combatants: they passed away, one by one – mainly drummer boys at the end – throughout the fifties and early sixties. By the 100th anniversary of Appomattox, there were no veterans of the conflict left to celebrate. America in 1965 had also moved on. It was celebrating civil rights, not the Civil War, and a new generation of Americans was in battle – "seeing the elephant", as Johnny Reb ad Billy Yank called it – in Vietnam.

In November 1998, the World War I allies celebrated the 80th anniversary of the armistice of the "War to End All Wars". No American veteran was able to come to France for the celebration. And no one who lived in France can forget the story of the last Senegalese veteran still living who was scheduled to get a French *Legion d'Honneur* on 11 November, 1998, but who died a day short, on the 10th. After eighty years, the veterans were almost all gone.

This year is the 60th anniversary of the onset of the liberation of France in World War II. It is being treated, as it should, as a major event: the leaders of the liberating nations and Germany will be attending. It is a celebration specifically of the events of 1944; it is also a celebration of the enormous and positive changes in relations between nations in Europe since the War. But, most of all, it is a celebration to honor those Allied veterans who spent years of their youth in the defense of freedom.

Those veterans are among those whom Hilary Kaiser sought out in her wonderful book *Veteran Recall*. This is an oral history of 17 people: most are American service members, but some are French resistants or even civilians caught up in the war. Each of their stories is fascinating. We are not hearing from famous generals or winners of the Medal of Honor, but from average citizens who were asked to perform certain duties "because there was a war on", who did them as best they could and then went home. For many of them, home became France – that is how the author came to know them. All except one give their names while telling their stories. However, in her chapter headings, Hilary Kaiser depicts them according to who they were: "The Medic", "Two French Boys", "The Gunner and Messenger", etc. Many were associated with D-Day and some will surely be attending this year's 60th anniversary. Some no longer can. Since the first printing of *Veteran Recall*, five of the 17 people she quotes in the book have left us. We have, however, thanks to the author, the stories and remembrances of "The Secret Agent", "The News Broadcaster", "The Tank Commander", "The WWI Veteran Under Arrest" and "The Soldier from Utah"; even though those who lived those particular stories are now gone. Without this book, their stories and the stories of those who are still with us would have been lost forever. Hilary Kaiser had the wisdom to record their individual memories. Because of her, these veterans' stories will survive the 60th, the 80th and even the 100th anniversaries of World War II and beyond. Their courage and perseverance in the face of war will be an inspiration for us and our children. This book, written in honor of average citizens serving their countries in dark times, is their celebration; they wholly deserve it.

James S. Dickey
Brigadier General, U.S. Army (Retired)

ACKNOWLEDGEMENTS

My heartfelt thanks go to the interviewees in this book. I am especially grateful to Phyllis Michaux, who encouraged me from the beginning to take on and complete this project.

I would also like to thank Georges Bernage and all his team at Editions Heimdal.

Note to the Second Edition

Ten years have elapsed since this book was first published. The stories in *Veteran Recall* have been shared with families and friends of both the interviewees and the interviewer, as well as with a larger audience in France and the U.S. After the book came out, some of the veterans and I gave talks together during celebrations in Normandy and Paris of the 50th anniversary of D-Day. And over the years we have kept in touch. Working together on this project certainly created a bond between us that has been strong and lasting.

As we now prepare to celebrate the 60th anniversary of D-Day, a few dear people in this book are in ill health, and, sadly, several others have passed away. Veterans Sim Copans, George Hook, Ridgway Knight and Julius Winter are no longer with us. Nor is Carolyn Dupuis, who wrote the piece on her Uncle George. Fortunately, their stories survive, both in print and in our minds and hearts.

Hilary Kaiser

Paris, March 2004

CONTENTS

INTRODUCTION

The idea for this book emerged in the course of a research project on the American presence in France. While interviewing three delightful American "senior citizens" who have lived in Paris for many years, I discovered that all three were war veterans and had come to France, in different capacities, during World War II.

My interest in their recollections of those years seemed to revive dormant memories. As we spoke, and as the tape turned, the past came alive for them and for me.

I was fascinated. My father never spoke to me about his experiences in the Pacific. And though I had read about the war, seen "The Longest Day" and visited the Normandy beaches, I had never actually sat down and *listened* to veterans' war stories before. The personal reminiscences of my interviewees, as well as the ways they related them, turned out to be as varied as their backgrounds and roles in the war. I enjoyed listening to their anecdotes, hearing their reactions, sharing in their feelings. I was also very impressed. Although what they described took place fifty or more years before our interviews, the memories of that time were still very much alive. A date or a place name might be missing, but the accounts were vivid and detailed.

From these first three interviews grew a project of collecting oral histories of Americans now living in France who took part in the last war. The 17 interviews I conducted are only a sampling, and an unscientifically-chosen one, at that. The first three veterans gave me names, and these people gave me the names of others. I have received additional names from friends. The list is still growing. There are a remarkable number of U.S. World War II veterans living in France today! I was also put in touch with three Frenchmen – one now an American citizen – who got to know U.S. soldiers during the war and who very much wanted to share their memories. Their personal accounts are included here as well. Finally, I heard Carolyn Dupuis read her piece about her uncle at a church Memorial Day service and was so touched that I asked her to let me publish it.

Some of the people I contacted did not wish to be interviewed. Their reasons – painful memories, ill health, timidity – were, of course, respected. Unfortunately, in one or two cases, my request for an interview arrived too late. Sadly, time is beginning to run out for many wartime participants and witnesses.

Except for one volunteer who sent me his account from the United States and for Carolyn Dupuis' uncle, I met personally with all the people in this book. Our interviews took place in Parisian cafés, or at their homes, where I often met their spouses, many of whom are French. I made many new friends – friends of my father's generation – who were kind, helpful and encouraging. In addition to sharing their memories with me, my interviewees showed me their souvenirs, lent me photographs and letters, and authorized me to use their published or unpublished poems. I could not be more grateful.

Memory is a funny thing. It comes back in fits and starts. It wanders to other subjects and then returns unbidden. It corrects itself. Not surprisingly, then, a transcribed interview often ran to twenty or thirty pages. I had to edit and condense. In so doing, I tried, as much as possible, to respect each person's voice. The final versions and the biographical information were all reviewed, as were the French to English translations, by the people interviewed. In a few cases, rereading the written text brought back more precise memories, and details had to be added. What is gained in precision may be at the loss of spontaneity, but who are we to judge?

Although this is a book of memories, not a historical document, the historical background is everywhere present: dates, places, and battles are all mentioned. I have tried to arrange the personal recollections in loose geographical and chronological order. While most of those interviewed lived through the war in France, and more particularly in Normandy, there are also recollections of North Africa, the South Pacific, England, Belgium, the Netherlands, Italy and Germany. In some cases, people moved from place to place or held more than one job. And people's stories and experiences sometimes intertwine.

From these personal stories emerge many compelling images: a six-foot-two sergeant wading ashore with his men at Utah Beach, a General losing his trousers in cold Algerian waters, an American medic treating a German soldier in a Norman church, a G.I. in Germany watching his buddy's head blown off by mortar shell, a commander crawling over to a burning tank to save one of his "boys", a 13-year old girl witnessing the execution of Yugoslav soldiers by a German firing squad, an information officer exchanging a Hershey bar for some fresh eggs, a counter intelligence man staring in horror at the piles of ashes outside a Dachau furnace room.

All of these images, plus many others, were part of the war. It was a time of combat, suffering, confusion, loss, destruction and horror. But it was often also a time of friendship, dedication, heroism, adventure, romance, suspense, and even comedy.

No war, of course, is a "good" war. And yet, despite the hardship and pain, I cannot help but think that some good did, in fact, come out of this war for the people who inhabit these stories. For four of them, it was an impetus to creativity, as their poems and musical pieces attest. For several, it was an occasion to meet a spouse. For almost all, it was the discovery of a new land which would later become their second home.

The people in this book lived through those wartime years . They recalled them "as if they were yesterday" or needed to garner them from the archives of their memories. Whichever the case, "You come out of such an experience forever basically changed," they said. Sixty years later, we nead their stories and try to understand. We imagine what it was like and empathize as best we can. Our hearts fill with fellow-feeling and gratitude towards these men and women – and others – for what they did those many years ago, and I personally feel honored that they agreed to share their remembrances with me.

CHRONOLOGY of WORLD WAR II

(EUROPEAN THEATER)

• **August 1939:** Germany invades Poland

• **September 1939:** France and Great Britain declare war on Germany

• **May 1940:** German subjugation of Denmark, Norway, Luxembourg, Holland, and Belgium

• **June 1940:** Italy declares war on France and Britain. France falls to Germany. Armistice signed. Division of France into several zones. French government established in Vichy under leadership of Marshal Pétain and Pierre Laval. French National Committee ("Free French") set up in London by General DeGaulle. Unsuccessful attempt by Free French to gain control of the navy and of African possessions. July 3, 1940, Britain destroys French naval vessels at Mers El-Kébir, near Oran, Algeria.

• **August 1940-April 1941:** Battle for Britain ("buzz bombs")

• **June 1941:** Hitler invades Russia

• **December 7, 1941:** Japanese bomb Pearl Harbor

• **December 8, 1941:** the United States declares war on Japan, and later on Italy and Germany

• **January 1942:** U.S. troops begin arriving in Britain

• **August 19, 1942:** Anglo-Canadian raid on Dieppe to test German defense

• **November 1942:** British General Montgomery and his 8th Army start offensive against German Marshal Rommel in North Africa. American and British forces land a few days later (Operation Torch). Capture of Casablanca and Oran.

- **November 1942:** German army invades "free zone" of France
- **November 27, 1942:** Sinking of French fleet in Toulon
- **May 1943:** Rommel defeated in North Africa
- **July 10, 1943:** Allies land in Sicily (Operation Husky)
- **September 8, 1943:** Surrender of Italy. Allies land in Italy (Operation Avalanche)
- **October 13, 1943:** Italy joins Allies and declares war on Germany
- **June 6, 1944:** Allies under General Dwight D. Eisenhower land in Normandy with 156,000 men in 4000 ships and an air cover of 11,000 airplanes (Operation Overlord)
- **July 31, 1944:** Allies, newly supported by U.S. 3rd Army under General Patton, break through German defenses at Avranches
- **August 6-8, 1944:** German counter-attack at Mortain
- **August 15, 1944:** U.S. 7th Army and French 1st Army land in Provence (Operation Anvil, later renamed Operation Dragoon)
- **August 24, 1944:** Liberation of Paris by French 2nd division under General Jacques Leclerc
- **August 31, 1944:** U.S. 3rd Army takes Verdun
- **September 1944:** Allies take Aachen and invade Germany
- **Novembre 23, 1944:** Liberation of Strasbourg by 2nd DB of General Leclerc
- **December 1944:** German counteroffensive at the Battle of the Bulge (Bastogne, Belgium)
- **February 8-11, 1945:** Roosevelt, Stalin and Churchill meet in Yalta to organize the end of the war, the occupation of Germany, the fate of Poland, and Russia's entering the war against Japan
- **March 1945:** Patton's 3rd Army reaches the Rhine at Coblenz
- **May 8, 1945:** Germany surrenders. End of the war in Europe.
- **August 1945:** U.S. drops atomic bombs on Hiroshima (August 6) and Nagasaki (August 9)
- **September 2, 1945:** Japan surrenders. End of World War II.

NORTH AFRICA

The secret agent

Grandson of D. Ridgway Knight and son of L. Aston Knight, two successful American artists who lived in France, Ridgway B. Knight was born in Paris in June 1911. After attending a French boarding school and the University of Paris, he obtained a Master's Degree from the Harvard Business School. Upon graduation in 1931, he began working in New York for Cartier, the famous jewelers, as special assistant to Pierre Cartier. Then in 1936, he and a friend took over Bellows and Company, a prestigious firm established in 1830 that imported fine wines and spirits into the United States. When Knight and his partner decided to join the war effort in the spring of 1941, the business was sold, and Knight was sent abroad.

Knight grew up in France, spoke perfect French and was very much of an interventionist even before the U.S. decided to join the war. During the winter of 1940-1941, he and his brother George set up "The Friends of Normandy" association to raise money to send to families living in the area of Beaumont-le-Roger, where the Knight family residence, a manor house built by Mansard with beautiful gardens as famous as Monet's, was located. Although married with three children, he felt very strongly that he should enlist. His attempts to get into the Air Force, Navy or Marine Corps proved futile, however, as it turned out that he was color blind!

His application came to the attention of the State Department, which sent him off to French North Africa on an intelligence mission with Ambassador Robert D. Murphy. Together with French Resistance groups, they prepared the November 8th, 1942 landings. The mission lasted from April 1941 to December 1942. He later served as a Major in the U.S. Army in Morocco, Italy and southern France from January 1943 to August 1945.

As the war was ending, Knight took a week off and typed out a hundred singled-spaced pages of notes, put them away and forgot them for 38 years. In the mid-1980s, he took them out again and produced a 307-page unpublished manuscript (entitled A Secret Affair: A Personal Account of the Preparation of the Landings in French-North Africa, November 1942) *to show to his family and friends. The book makes for fascinating reading.*

President Roosevelt had been Assistant Secretary of the Navy during part of the First World War and had a geopolitical sense, in addition to being greatly interested in the French fleet. Thus, he realized, from the outset of World War II, that North Africa would be a valuable jumping-off place for operations against the Axis, so he inquired as to what intelligence we had about French North Africa. It turned out that the consulates there had not even sent over to Washington phone books of the major cities! The U.S. needed to know more about Algeria, Morocco and Tunisia. We needed to be in touch with people there and to ascertain the state of mind of the officials and the military.

This was the origin of the "Twelve Apostles' Mission" to North Africa. Although there were actually only eleven of us "vice-consuls", we came to be known by some as "the Twelve Apostles", hence the name. Our diplomatic mission was put together and masterminded by Bob Murphy, Counselor of the U.S. Embassy in Vichy. He and General Maxime Weygand, who at the time was the French Pro-Consul in North Africa, worked out an agreement in March 1941 whereby we would help the French in maintaining peace and quiet among the local populations by supplying them with tea, sugar, and cotton cloth. In return, the French would permit us to send over twelve vice consuls and technical advisors to make sure that these supplies would not be shipped across the Mediterranean to France, where they might be used by the Germans. This, in fact, was the cover under which the eleven of us went over in May 1941.

As I say in my book, I have never lived as intensively or as excitingly as I did during those 20 months I spent in Algeria. From a wine merchant and family-man, I found myself a secret agent in a conspiracy that would prepare for the November 1942 landings and pave the way to our winning the war. In connection with my appointment, however, I must stress that at no time did I belong to the O.S.S., which did not exist when we were sent to North Africa.

One of the most exciting experiences I had during that time was helping to organize the Cherchell Conferece. It was, in fact, a clandestine meeting between General Mark Clark, Chief of Staff to General Eisenhower, accompanied by four of his staff officers, and a group of French Resistance leaders, both military officers and civilians, with whom we had been working in North Africa. The meeting was to take place in a lonely farmhouse in Cherchell, about 120 kilometers west of Algiers, on the road to Oran. Bob Murphy had asked me to accompany him and had placed me in charge of the logistics of the operation. The visitors were to come from Gibraltar by British submarine and arrive during the night of October 20th, 1942.

Unfortunately, however, the submarine only reached the rendezvous at daylight, and the meeting had to be postponed until the night of the 21st, which meant contacting each French participant individually and making many changes. The visitors did arrive, however, and the talks took place, only to be curtailed by the news of the imminent arrival of a squad of soldiers and the local Commissioner of Police, who had been tipped off about some unusual happenings going on at the estate!

The French conferees left for Algiers in their cars in considerable confusion. We hid General Clark, his four staff officers and three British commandos, in a wine cellar under the living-room floor. Bob Murphy, Jacques Teissier, who was our host, another man and I began playing poker on a table which we'd placed over the trap-door to the cellar. Fifteen minutes later one of our men stationed outside knocked on the door and said the Police Commissioner was there and wanted to speak to someone in authority. Bob Murphy looked at me, so I went. It wasn't easy, but I was able to convince the Commissioner nothing too serious was wrong. I pretended that Monsieur Murphy, an American Counselor of Embassy and my superior, and I were two bachelors alone in Algeria who had arranged for a rendez-vous with two Algerian ladies of good families in this secluded spot. If the Commissioner went on with his investigation, it might become very unpleasant for everyone concerned and create a diplomatic incident!

After the Commissioner and his military escort had headed off up the road, we decided we had to get General Clark and the others back to the submarine in the kayaks they'd come ashore in. But it was still daylight, there was a strong wind and the waves were very high. We waited until around 9 o'clock and tried to launch the kayaks, but they kept overturning. We tried again at midnight, but with no luck. Finally, around 4:30 a.m., the wind fell, and we made another attempt. Four of us stripped naked and did our best to lift the kayaks above the waves. We finally got General Clark and his men safely off to the submarine, which had come in dangerously close to shore.

Just as the sun was coming up in the east, we finished cleaning up the beach, picking up everything our visitors had taken off to lighten themselves and the kayaks. Trousers, field jackets, weapons and the like. The story about General Clark's lost trousers became quite famous when it appeared in the press and cartoons later on!

We returned to Algiers that day. I slept all the way through till the next afternoon, but awoke in excessive pain. The long stay in the water at Cherchell, as well as the cold and the wind, had caused abscesses in both my ears. These abscesses evolved rapidly, and I found myself with two broken eardrums. Although my left ear later healed, I have been permanently deaf in my right ear ever since.(...)

After the landings on November 8th, 1942, I felt a terrible let-down because for two years I had been working with one hopeful objective, and that was, of course, the liberation of North Africa. And when something you've wanted for some time comes about there *is* a terrible letdown. For the first few days after the landings, I didn't care much what happened. Then came the question of what I was going to do. Bob Murphy paid me the compliment of asking me to come on his permanent staff in Algiers but I hadn't left my family and joined the war to sit in an office in Algiers. So instead of that, I accepted General Clark's solicitation to join his staff. He remembered me from the Cherchell adventure and knew I had knowledge of North Africa and was bilingual in French.

General Clark had been given command of an Army which was to be created, the 5th Army, and he had decided that the best place for this was in Eastern Morocco. He needed a liaison officer with the

French authorities in Rabat – Morocco being a French protectorate at the time. So, after I had been commissioned as a Major in the Army, he sent me as the liaison officer of the 5th Army to the French Resident General, General Noguès. I stayed in Rabat for seven months and found General Noguès most cooperative, which was surprising because at the time of the landings he had held out for three days against our landing forces. Obviously he was trying to make up.

What I remember with the greatest pleasure about that time was an extraordinary trip around Morocco which General Noguès took General Clark and me on. It was done in a style which only an absolute ruler can do. For example when we landed in Casablanca, we drove from the airport to the middle of town on a road not only lined with troops, but also lined with the population. And since in a Muslim country the women are not supposed to demonstrate out-of-doors, the bourgeois ladies in Casablanca were represented by their slave girls holding dummies, large dolls, representing their mistresses, over the heads of the crowd. It made quite a sight. First the troops, then lines of Moroccan men cheering, and then behind them these huge dolls peering over the crowd. We went on into the country where a huge Fantasia was organized. Several hundred Moroccan horsemen came charging at us and then stopped at the last moment. I also remember an amphitheater, with 13,000-15,000 tribesmen lining the hills forming this amphitheater. It was colonial Morocco – something which will probably never be repeated there.

The French were rather distrustful of American ambitions at first, thinking we wanted to succeed them after the war. So whenever I saw a Moroccan official, I was accompanied by a French chaperone. But with time, I gained the confidence of the French and was able to see the Sultan, Mohammed the 5th, twice by myself. This was most unusual, indeed!

General De Gaulle came over and became the political chief in North Africa in, as I remember, April of '43. This meant that General Noguès was cashiered, and in June a representative of the Free French political line, Ambassador Gabriel Puaux, was appointed to succeed him. I was quite amused that our Free French allies proved to be much more difficult to deal with than General Noguès, who had fought against us previously.

The Sicilian operation was just about to take place and General Clark and his army would be leaving Morocco to take part in active war, which meant that my job disappeared with it. As much as General Clark had thought he needed me in North Africa, it was clear that he felt he wouldn't need me in Italy, since at that time I spoke no Italian and had no connections. I was assigned to the staff of General Edgar Erskine Hume, who was to be the military commander of the liberated part of Italy.

I landed in Salerno on D-Day, plus five, D-Day having been September 8th, which is when the Armistice we had negotiated with the Italians took effect. The landing had actually been very difficult. (...) When I landed, General Clark saw me and said, "Gentlemen, there is Ridgway Knight. Our luck has turned." I guess he considered me an omen of good luck after what had happened at Cherchell.

During this time I gradually wound up at Ravello on the Sorrento peninsula in the Salerno mountains performing various odd jobs on General Hume's staff. I then received an assignment to get General Hume to the *municipio*, the town hall, of Naples, as early as possible. This was on September 28th or 29th. In any event, the next day the Germans were retreating and were close to the outskirts of Naples, and we decided to make a dash of it on the morning of October 1st. We were in the Hotel Caruso in Ravello, and on the night of September 30th there was a very noisy table in the restaurant consisting of officers of the King's Dragoon Guards, a British élite outfit. At the end of the dinner we got together and made a bet as to who would get to the town hall first. The bet was a good dinner in Naples. The next morning with the sergeant, General Hume, two jeeps, and six enlisted men, we made our way through the tanks and the cheering crowds of Italians throwing flowers on us. But as we got closer, there were fewer and fewer tanks and fewer and fewer Italians on the streets. I had a detailed street map of Naples. The Germans had evacuated, but there were still snipers around. We made our way through the back streets and got to the town hall at 8:30 a.m. on October 1st. I'm proud to say we beat the King's Guards by an hour. Recently, however, I read an official book on Naples that said the Dragoon Guards were the first unit to make it into Naples, arriving at 9:30 a.m. I felt very cheated!

The adventure was only starting. General Hume, a polished and charming elderly gentleman who liked society and spoke fluent Italian, was delighted to be in Naples. And as we arrived at the *municipio*, some Italians, recognizing the American jeeps, came out, and Hume decided to stay with them. He told me to go into the town hall. I was met by an usher, who marched me up to the offices of the acting mayor of Naples. The mayor stood up and said very formally, "Signore Officer, this desk is yours." So, in a way, you could say that by accident I received the surrender of Naples!

About an hour after I had sat down at the desk of the mayor, six or seven bedraggled Italian officers, who had taken refuge in the cellars of the *municipio* when the Germans recaptured Naples after the signing of the armistice, marched into my office. They included an Admiral and the General of the Carabinieri. They more or less snapped to attention, and the spokesman said, "*Signore Maggiore, che facciamo noi?*" So, I said the first thing to do was to "*sgomberare le strade*," to clean the streets. Naples was a mess. The Carabiniere said, "That, sir, is not the work of the Carabinieri." "Well, unfortunately, sir, it is today," I replied.

Not only were the streets cleaned, but they also discovered more than a hundred trucks, hidden away here and there, which turned out to be most useful for supplying the civilian needs of Naples.

I don't mean to seem immodest, but I remember a musical tribute paid to me for my contribution towards meeting the needs of the Neapolitans while I was in Naples. Before the war, there was a very popular song called "Night and Day". My closest associate in Naples was a certain Lt. Colonel Kraege. One evening, while I was dining in a Neapolitan restaurant, I happened to be serenaded by a group singing, "Knight and Kraege, you are the ones...."!

My work in Naples proved to be very interesting, as I was later given the responsibility for dealing with the political parties in the city. I then received an assignment to the Anzio beachhead, which was surrounded by the Germans and which remained a static front.

A memory that I have of Anzio is of Italian Prince Borghese, who was *the* landlord in the area. Even though he was a long time fascist, he had decided that his duty was to remain with his peasants and his tenants. He was, in other words, a man whom I respected.

During the several weeks I stayed in Anzio, I dined with him several times in his palace, and I must say I was struck and amused by the extraordinary contrast between the formal dinners in the beautifully decorated dining room – the perfect service and the choice wines – and what was going on outside.

By that time it was early April, and General Clark was planning for the attack on Rome. By then, the French Expeditionary Corps, consisting of four divisions of North African veterans and com- manded by a remarkable soldier, General Juin, had joined the 5th Army. With this strong French component in the 5th Army, General Clark suddenly remembered Major Knight. So I was yanked out of civil affairs and brought back to 5th Army Headquarters, where I become personal liaison officer between General Clark and General Juin. I was in for a most interesting few months. The French forces were remarkable. They had in their hearts a desire to vindicate French arms and they did. General Juin, his staff, his men, and the Moroccan Irregulars, put on their best show. They did such an extraordinary job that when we finally arrived in Rome, General Clark insisted on having General Juin arrive with him in his jeep and said in a loud voice, "General, without you we wouldn't be here."

Notwithstanding General Clark's well-known egocentrism, he was sincerely in admiration of General Juin and of the extraordinary performance of the French Expeditionary Corps – especially the Moroccan Goums – in turning the German defenses north of Cassino along mountains which the Germans thought impassable. When – unfortunately because of General DeGaulle's hostility – the French Expeditionary was withdrawn from Italy, transformed into the French 1st Army and entrusted to General de Lattre de Tassigny, General Clark asked me to draft a tribute to the French performance in Italy. What was my surprise, and pleasure, to find this text in a biography of General Juin as one of the tributes of which he was proudest.

After we captured Rome, the progression was much easier, and I remember we had a flood of distinguished visitors, including General Marshall, our Chief of Staff. On that occasion there was a near drama. General Marshall prided himself on speaking good French, which was not at all the case. At one moment during the briefing, General Juin got up and said in French, "I will now give

General Marshall an *exposé* on where the British..." Hearing this, General Marshall exploded and said "Damn it! I'm not going to sit here and listen to some Frenchman exposing our best allies!" He didn't realize that *exposé* in French means a summary, not an "exposure"! I was the interpreter for this occasion, and attempted to tell him but he silenced me with, "Young man, I know my French!" It was only with great difficulty that General Clark and I succeeded in having General Marshall refrain from challenging General Juin publicly.

Another distinguished visitor was George VI of England, who had come to decorate some of our men. I remember after the ceremony, when we were having lunch, General Clark's sergeant, who was the steward, became very flustered because he didn't know how to address the King. I suddenly heard this very dark, smiling man say, "Yes, your Highness...Your Majesty... Sir!" General De Gaulle came for two visits. As we all know, De Gaulle was very proud of the French language and always spoke it. But once in a conversation he got confused and spoke to me, the interpreter, in English, for me to translate into French!

As June wore on, the French command got word from Algiers that a good part of the French corps would have to leave immediately to prepare itself for the landings in the south of France. I remember quite well one conversation between General Clark and General Juin, as I was his interpreter then. General Clark asked if Juin expected the *entire* French corps to be drawn away. Juin said yes and soon. General Clark expressed his hope that General Juin would be given the command. Juin replied that he didn't think that would be the case. He clearly implied that with De Gaulle around, he would not be given the post, as this later proved to be true.

Well, having heard of the upcoming operation in France, I asked General Clark for a favor: to be assigned to a unit landing in France. He very kindly consented. I'll always remember Colonel Charles Salzman, the Deputy Chief of Staff, running over to me in the hospital, where I was being treated for a slight injury, and saying, "Ridgway, you've got it! You're to go ashore with the 15th Infantry of the 3rd division. General Clark is getting in touch with General Patch." Well the result was that I landed on D-Day, August 15th, in southern France, just back of St. Tropez, which, that day, was quite deserted! I came ashore two hours after the first wave. German resistance was, on the whole, fairly light, and we just had to clean up a few points along the beach.

My first contact with a Frenchman was something I'll always remember. I was making my way up a ditch, along the side of a small road, when I came upon a French *paysan*, who was busily hoeing his vineyards. I couldn't restrain myself and so I shouted out: "*Alors, ça va ?*" He straightened up, looked at me and simply said: "*Monsieur l'officier, ça va mieux.*" And with that he bent over his hoe and continued working! And I'd always thought that the people in southern France, the *Midi,* were particularly garrulous and prone to making long speeches!

Operation Anvil, the name of this landing in southern France, came to me as an anti-climax after the experiences I'd had in North Africa before the landings and in Italy. As the result of General Clark's message to General Patch, who was commanding the 7th Army, I was assigned, after the landings, as liaison officer with the French on General Patch's staff. The first thing I had to do was write citations for the French Resistance leaders who had given us a hand at the time of the landing. I must say that this gave an insight on what the Resistance was, and later became. The outfit that had given us help was called the *Batallion des Maures*, the Maures being a low chain of mountains near the seaside. In all, the battalion consisted of 80 men. And when three days after the landings we decorated a few Resistance leaders, the number of resistants on the *Place* of St. Tropez was about 800, no longer just 80! This was pretty typical of the situation pervading in France, where there were probably a hundred times more people claiming to have been Resistants than those who actually endangered themselves.

For political reasons, it had been decided that the French First Army, which landed two days after we did, would be given the route up the Rhône Valley and through the French cities, Lyon and so on. The reason was that we wanted the French flag, the *tricolore,* to be shown in these towns. We wanted them to be liberated by French forces and thought this would be healthy for French morale, which had been damaged by the defeat and occupation. Our road was the none-too-easy *route Napoléon* through the Alps and Grenoble.

General Patch very kindly arranged for me to accompany him up to Paris on a two-day leave. He knew of my interest in France and that I had lived in Paris and Normandy. Paris was liberated on August 25th. We must have arrived there about September 5th or 6th. I had two marvelous days in Paris, and I'll always remember them. The monuments, the clouds, the beautiful girls and women in flowered skirts riding bicycles. It made an absolutely heavenly sight. I also remember one of my meals there. It was at Prunier's. The Normandy coast had been liberated, so there were oysters, but there were no lemons available in Paris and we were given vinegar to put on them. Also at that time...I had an uncle who'd stayed in France during the war. He had first been interned and then led a very quiet life. I called on him, and he informed me that our family place in Normandy had been destroyed.

While on our way north, I happened to write a dispatch on the conditions I observed going through the countryside and towns and after speaking to French people. As it turns out, this report had a determining effect on my subsequent life. It happened to get handed over to Jefferson Caffery, just as he was leaving the States in early October to become our first Ambassador to France following the liberation. It seems my report was the only one in the briefing papers given Caffery dealing with the situation south of the Loire, and he exclaimed, "I want that Major on my staff."

But before I went to work for the State Department, I was assigned, with two English officers, to conduct a tactical reconnaissance of some of the German pockets on the Atlantic. When the Germans retreated from western France, they held out around seaports which they thought could be of use to us : Cherbourg, Lorient, St. Nazaire, La Rochelle, and – in order to close the port of Bordeaux – the Pointe de Graves. This expedition proved a fascinating experience, giving me the chance to observe the disorganization that reigned in this period after the landing, when the French government had not yet taken over control. It became clear to me that the settling of personal accounts all too often led to executions, which were, in fact, assassinations. I don't think anyone knows exactly how many people were liquidated during this period, but the estimates vary between 20,000 and 50,000. This is a chapter in French history about which little has been written.

This was in late October, early November. It happened that I was the first American in uniform in Bordeaux, which rather pleased me, due to my former wine connections and ongoing interest. I had a glorious stay there with one of the wine dignitaries whom I knew from before the war, Jacques Calvet. I stayed with him for three nights, getting up at 4:30 a.m. to go on reconnaissance missions to the Pointe de Graves and returning in the evening. We had the most wonderful wine tastings. Famous twin years, such as 1899 and 1900, and I must say that they were some of the best *magnums* I have ever drunk. These wines had never been moved from their cellar of origin. Hence, they were in absolutely perfect condition.

In early December, about four weeks after returning to Paris, I was informed of my assignment to the American Embassy in Paris...

Following the war, Knight remained in uniform for a year, having been assigned to the U.S. Embassy in Paris as Special Assistant to Ambassador Jefferson Caffery. He then became a civilian employee of the Embassy and later joined the Foreign Service. His career with the State Department would include assignments in Washington, Germany and Pakistan. He served in Paris from 1955-1957 as Political Advisor to the NATO Supreme Commander. From 1960-1973 he was U.S. Ambassador to Syria, Belgium and Portugal. In 1973 he became Director of International Relations of the Chase Manhattan Bank reporting directly to David Rockefeller, but based in Paris.

Retired since 1982, Ambassador Knight was a very active member of the American community in Paris. He was president of the American Club from June 1984 to June 1989. He was on the Boards of Directors of the American Friends of Blérancourt, the Fulbright Commission for France and Friends of Vieilles Maisons Françaises. A long-time connoisseur of French wines, he was a member of the Academy of French Wine and did research on Thomas Jefferson's years in Paris and, more especially, his interest in wines.

Like his grandfather and his father before him, Ambassador Knight was honored by the French Legion d'Honneur. Because of a most infrequent – if not unique – mistake, he was twice named "Chevalier": in 1944 for his military service in Italy and the fol-

lowing year for his work as a former vice-consul in preparing the North African landings. In 1991, he was finally promoted to "Officier". He was also the recipient of the U.S. Medal for Merit, the Bronze Star, the Croix de Guerre, the Italian Medal for Valor and the Medal of Merit of the Order of Malta.

Knight's great regret was the loss of the family home and his father's atelier *in Beaumont-le-Roger. It is one of the ironies of the war that they were destroyed by the U.S. Air Force when General Patton was effecting his breakthrough near Avranches in August 1944. Knight believed news of the destruction helped precipitate the death of his father, who was in the United States at the time. The house had also had "visitations" before being devastated: Neighbors had helped themselves to the paintings in the atelier and the German Air Force had lived there for awhile.*

Ambassador Knight died in August 2001. He is survived by his French wife, Christine, his four American sons by two deceased former wives, and numerens grandchildren and great grandchildren. Ambassador Knight lived on and off in France for many years, appreciated French food and wine and had many French friends. Nevertheless, he considered himself a full-fledged American and was proud of the fact that three of his grandparents arrived on the shores of North America before 1700, and the fourth a few years later.

SOUTH PACIFIC

The naval officer

Born in Winnfield, Louisiana in 1918, William Jay Smith grew up at Jefferson Barracks, just south of St. Louis on the Mississippi. His father was an enlisted man, a clarinetist in the Sixth Infantry Band, and the family lived on the Missouri army base for the twenty years between the wars. After going to public schools in St. Louis, Smith attended Washington University and received both a B.A. degree and a Master's degree in French. His first experience living in France dates back to the summer of 1938, when he spent several months studying French at the Institut de Touraine in Tours.

Smith enlisted in the Navy in the summer of 1941 and entered the V-7 Officers Training Program in January 1942, just after the attack on Pearl Harbor. A "ninety-day wonder" of a crash program at Northwestern University, he received his commission as an ensign and orders to report to Pearl Harbor in June 1942. There he was reunited briefly with his father, who had been stationed at Schofield Barracks during the Japanese attack.

After a few months on Oahu, he was assigned as communications officer, and afterwards personnel officer, to a naval air base on the island of Palmyra, a thousand miles southwest of Honolulu. Ten months later, probably because of his language ability and background in French, Italian and Spanish, he was transferred to Casablanca. In January 1944 he was named liaison officer on board the French sloop La Grandière and sailed to the South Pacific.

Although he had written poetry throughout college and had had his first poem published in a national magazine when he was seventeen, Smith believes his career as a writer really began while he was on board La Grandière. He wrote several war poems during that time and sent them off to the New Republic and Poetry Magazine from various ports of call. Most of them were published, and a group *of them entitled "Dark Valentine" poems, received a prize from* Poetry *in 1945. In addition, Smith was one of the youngest poets to be included in Oscar Williams' anthology,* The War Poets. *While on board ship, Smith also began his work as a translator of foreign poets: his translations of Louis Aragon's "Les Yeux d'Elsa" were published during this period.*

The poems "Convoy" and "Columbus Circle Swing" included here are from the "Dark Valentine" group and were written aboard La Grandière *in 1944-1945.*

Convoy

The ships are fitted, and the convoy sails;
our course is toward the east and to the sun.
Antennae turn, our only contact whales;
we seek the Jonah who inhabits one.
Airborne the continents above us meet,
below lie cities which we lean to hear.
The sea unwinds like the ends of Easy Street,
where no one goes straight but all will come out in the clear.

Not like the islander with outrigged craft,
nor Jack who journeyed high upon the bean,
have we for long days roamed the decks and laughed
aboard these liberties! I do not mean
we have been comfortable, nor for that matter, clean.
Ask the man struck dead by the lifeboat somewhere aft.

WILLIAM JAY SMITH

I got orders to go from Palmyra Island all the way to Casablanca. This was shortly after the landings in 1943. First I went back to the States, then by troop ship to Oran. Twenty-odd days in the hold of a Liberty Ship in a large, slow-moving convoy is not the pleasantest way to travel, but I like being at sea and am never sea-sick. I discovered, as many others before me had, that the worst feature of military life is the hours of sheer tedium with which one is constantly confronted. But I was never bored: at idle moments I went over and over in my head experiences and memories that eventually found their way into my poems.

From Oran, along with ten other naval officers, I went through the Atlas mountains by boxcar on those old narrow-guage tracks. It was during Ramadan. The cars were filled with Moroccan and Algerian troops, who didn't eat during the day. So when the sun went down, the train had to stop in these little villages. A gun would be fired and the troops would get off, build fires along the track, and eat. I was the only one among the Americans who spoke French: the villagers would gather round and I'd interpret. Now when I hear about places like Sidi-bel-Abbès, the headquarters of the French Foreign Legion, I can remember very well how they looked at sundown.

I spent some three months in Casablanca as a communications officer, going up and down to Rabat and Port Lyautey every week as a courier. The American Navy had taken over one of the modern buildings at the center of Casablanca and this is where we officers lived and worked, cut off from the rest of the city, which had then returned to normal after the landings. But I was reminded of the action that had taken place there when I went for lunch with French officers on the *Jean Bart*, the battleship that had been badly damaged. Isolated as we were in our military enclave, I got to know little of Morocco, although I visited regularly a number of French families.

In January 1944 I replaced the British liaison officer on the aviso colonial, *La Grandière*. It had been built as a patrol vessel, or gunboat, for use in the French colonies. Three hundred fifty feet in length, it had three five-inch guns and a special apartment for a visiting governor. It was quite elegantly fitted out. I had far more pleasant quarters than I would have had on an American ship. *La Grandière* had fought against the Americans in Casablanca. Afterwards, a British officer had been on board as a liaison officer, and the ship had escorted convoys up and down the African coast between Dakar and Casablanca. Then the French Admiralty asked that it be sent to join the American fleet in the South Pacific so as to be in touch with the French colonies there. I replaced the British officer, since I was the only American officer around who spoke French.

We crossed the north Atlantic in January in terrible weather at a very dangerous time. It took us twenty-one days. We were one of the transports of a convoy of some thirty ships, and because we had little speed, we were towards the back. I was in charge of the ship's communications; I had all the secret codes, and my men – a radioman and two signalmen – and I would be up all night deciphering them.

When we were several days out and I had just crawled into my bunk at dawn, one of the French sailors rushed into my cabin to tell me with great urgency that the captain wanted me at once on the bridge. I pulled on my pants as I struggled as quickly as possible up through the dark. Once on the bridge, I was handed by the captain a message that had just been flashed from one of the cargo vessels in the convoy. It read: MATE, ARE YOU A NEW KIND OF SHIP OR WHAT? The captain wanted to know what he should reply and was unhappy when I told him to ignore this silly inquiry, which was in dangerous violation of the rules of the convoy, especially coming as it did at dawn. The captain could simply not understand how any message could go unanswered and called me a total incompetent in no uncertain terms. But when later that morning the signalmaster of the ship sent an apology, the captain decided that I wasn't quite as stupid as I had seemed.

The French officers were admirers of Darlan and Pétain and had photographs of them in their cabins, and naturally they were not very pleased to have me on board. In the beginning they really resented my presence. They treated me very coldly – properly, but coldly. This, of course, was easy enough to do because when they resorted to using French Navy slang, I couldn't understand a word they said. I was fairly fluent in French, but the slang was incomprehensible, as it would have been to any ordinary Frenchman. As time went by, though, and especially after we got to the States, we all became good friends. There must have been a couple of hundred men in the crew from all over France, a good many from Brittany, which has always produced sea-faring men, and they had all been away from home for a long time. The ship had become their only home.

The men in my liaison party had volunteered for the assignment when they heard that the ship was going to the States, but they were all miserable on board. Speaking not a word of French, they felt totally isolated; they detested their cramped quarters, the food, everything. They were determined not to continue on to the Pacific, and I was just as determined to get rid of them, which I managed to do when the ship was being reequipped in Norfolk only by making a direct appeal to the Office of Personnel in Washington. Just before we sailed, they were replaced by three French-speaking, excellently trained New Englanders, who had requested just such an assignment.

After making our way through the Panama Canal, we stopped first at the Marquesas Islands, where no French ship had been for a very long time, and for me this was one of the high points of my time on board. I was able to spend one day on the island of Nukuhiva, and to travel by horseback up the mountain over the ruins of ancient Polynesian temples and to gaze out on the valley that Herman Melville describes in *Typee*. Another day on the island of Hivaoa, where Gauguin had spent his last years, I visited his grave and met several of his Polynesian descendants. The *La Grandière* then sailed to Tahiti, on to Noumea in New Caledonia and Espiritu Santo in the New Hebrides. For some months we were the station ship at Espiritu Santo, and, at the request of the French Admiralty, made a tour of the other islands in the New Hebrides, which was then a British-French condominium. Afterwards we went on to Guadalcanal, Tulagi, Manus, and Funafuti, usually escorting cargo ships along the way.

Although my assignment on the *La Grandière*, meant being stuck in terrible heat for months in far-off places, it was, on the whole, not unpleasant. Among Americans in the South Pacific Fleet we became known as "the floating cocktail lounge" because, unlike American ships, we could have wine and liquor on board. Our wardroom had been elegantly fitted out for the colonies with leather banquettes, and we were served by a chef who accomplished miracles with American supplies; his sauces transformed cans of spam and Vienna sausages into unidentifiable but delectable dishes.

I was the first American naval officer in World War II to be assigned to a French ship, although later there were several involved in the landings in the south of France. In Norfolk when we were being refitted, the Navy Yard placed a telephone in my cabin and all communications addressed to the ship came first to me. Later in the South Pacific I accompanied the French captain when he reported to the admiral or captain in charge of the American bases. Going through the Panama Canal I stood between the French captain and the canal pilot, not an easy place to be as it turned out. According to French Navy regulations, the captain of a ship can never relinquish command of his vessel, but according to Panama Canal regulations, a captain must turn over control to the canal pilot. There were some tense moments when the pilot would give one order and the captain another. Anger mounted on both sides and I was caught between the two men trying to get them to understand each other.

I had some less tense and more relaxed experiences as interpreter. The natives on the island of Funafuti gave a big party honoring the officers of *La Grandière*, a splendid banquet and a series of dances, one of which dramatically enacted the Polynesian version of the Jonah story. The chief made a graceful speech of welcome which a young man beside him translated into English, then I turned his English into French. The French captain replied, but being a poor public speaker, he hesitated, beginning every sentence with the phrase, *en tout cas*. The first time I translated this as *In any case*, the second time as *Anyhow*, but the third and fourth time I simply omitted it. My French colleagues, carefully following both languages, took me to task afterwards for what they jokingly called my willful and unnecessary distortions of the captain's splendid text.

It was fortunate indeed that our months of tedious routine were broken more than once by Gallic wit. Jokes abounded about the cats the crew had taken aboard, a new one in each port of call and named for it – so that we had Norfolk, Panama, Tahiti, Noumea and so on. The captain had no objections to these acquisitions: he had two magnificent Siamese of his own – Thai and Poussao. When I opened the door of his cabin in Casablanca to present my orders, the cats flew at me, reducing my orders to shreds. A year later in Guadalcanal when the captain left to return to France, he made arrangements for Thai and Poussao to be taken to a planter in the New Hebrides. But on the way there, the cats made their displeasure known by hiding in dark places between the decks and howling incessantly. There is no sound more desolate than the pounding of waves in a heavy sea accompanied by the howling of lonely, abandoned cats. I hear them still sometimes when I wake up in the middle of the night.

The new captain detested cats, and, once the Siamese were delivered to their new owner, he ordered us to get rid of all the other cats on board at the next port. That proved to be the island of Manus, where we entered a harbor filled with hundreds of ships of every size and description, all preparing for the battle of Leyte in the Philippines. The ship's Supply Officer, Legoux, a little man with horn-rimmed glasses who looked exactly like Harold Lloyd, and I got into a boat, and one after another – Norfolk, Panama, Tahiti – the cats were handed down to us. But the officer in charge at the dock refused to let us take the cats ashore without special permission. While Legoux waited in the boat with his charges, which were, of course, becoming more and more desperate, I made the rounds of the huge base seeking that permission, but could find no officer anywhere willing to give it. I returned in desperation to the officer on the dock. He finally said that he could not give us any authorization but was willing to look the other way while we took the cats to the warehouses adjoining the dock, which we did. And there we let them loose.

Duty on *La Grandière* was far from perilous: on a number of occasions we pursued what proved to be non-existent Japanese submarines but we never saw any real action. All the same, I had two very narrow escapes: the difference, in one instance, of a few hours, in the other, of a few seconds, and I would not have been here to tell my story. We had been tied up for several days next to an ammunition ship at Guadalcanal when suddenly and unexpectedly we received orders in the middle of the night to depart to escort a cargo ship. We sailed at dawn and a few hours later the ammunition ship blew up, and with it, the entire dock. Another time, in Espiritu Santo, the officers of an American training submarine, whom I had met ashore, invited me to accompany them on one of their regular runs. I was standing with the captain in the conning tower of the submarine when he spotted a plane from an incoming American carrier headed down on us. Within seconds he had the submarine, which the pilot had mistaken for a Japanese one, deep underwater. Although it shook like a battered cocktail shaker from the impact of the bombs, it managed to struggle back to port. This was my first, and only, venture on a submarine.

After the war, Smith studied for a year (1947-1948) at Oxford as a Rhodes scholar and for two years in Italy. For mcny years he was a university professor, first of French at Washington University and then of English at Columbia University, Williams College and Hollins College. He was Chairman of the Writing Division of the School of the Arts, Columbia University, 1973-1975. Smith is a well-known poet and translator of foreign poetry. He has published over fifty books, including collections of poetry, a memoir of his youth entitled Army Brat, *children's books, several collections of criticism and translations from French, Spanish, Italian, Russian, Hungarian and Swedish. He is currently working on a semi-autobiographical novel set in Touraine during the summer of 1938.*

Smith is the recipient of many awards for his writing. He was Consultant in Poetry to the Library of Congress (a post now called Poet Laureate) from 1968-1970 and has been a member of the American Academy of Arts and Letters since 1975. He has received two medals from the Hungarian government for his translations of Hungarian poetry. In 1992 he was awarded the Médaille de Vermeil by the French Academy for his translations of French poetry. He has also received several awards for his children's books.

Smith and his French wife, Sonja Haussmann, a translator in her own right, who translated a selection of her husband's poems, L'Arbre du Voyageur *in 1992, live half of the year in western Massachusetts and the other half in Paris. Smith finds life in the French capital far less hectic than in New York; he takes the subway everywhere and does a lot of walking. He spends much time at the Bibliothèque Nationale and in bookstores and museums. He says he feels more in touch with the rest of the world here than he does in New York because of the closeness of other European capitals and of Africa. According to him, a number of other American writers have settled in Paris for several months a year, and they now form a small colony. Smith has also quite a few connections with French writers, among them Alain Bosquet, who translated a selection of his poems,* Primitif Américain, *in 1993 and Michel Déon, of the French Academy, whom Smith met in 1990 at an international writers' festival in Toronto.*

Columbus Circle Swing

Old Mr. Christopher sailed an egg
to prove that it was round
while the man at the keg with the wooden leg
stood his ground.

Brothers Wright, perfecting flight,
let the rabbit out of the hat:
Now overhead the quadruped
disputes his habitat.

O where shall we go when it rains all the day,
and what shall we do when it's over:
will the day be as bright when it dawns at Calais
as it was after dark at Dover?

Bombers roar off overhead
turn down your shaded lamps.
The cities burn, a Christmas red,
smoke rises from the camps.

The world's an egg, ah, through and through.
It was decided for us.
You can always change a line or two;
you cannot change the chorus.

O where shall we go when it rains all the day,
and what shall we do when it's over:
will the day be as bright when it dawns at Calais
as it was after dark at Dover?

WILLIAM JAY SMITH

NORMANDY

The medic

Born in Lewiston, Maine, Roger Lantagne came to France for the first time by way of the sky, jumping into Normandy on D-Day with the 101st Airborne Division.

"When a soldier goes through something like that, you don't forget. It seems like we landed this morning," he says, pulling out a worn photograph of a group of 14 buddies beneath the wing of a glider. It is the only wartime photograph he has . All the others were stolen, along with his bags, when he returned to Fort Devon, Massachusetts in 1945.

As might be expected, Normandy remains a special place for Lantagne, who came to retire in France in 1973. Being a D-Day veteran, he says he has always been welcomed in Normandy as a son or a brother, even though the Americans demolished people's homes and villages. For him, the ties, which go beyond mere friendship, are still there, even 50 years later.

When I was in high school, I used to work as a volunteer in the hospital of my home town. I'd take care of patients and whatever had to be done. But when I went into the Service in 1942, the Army wanted to put me in with the engineers. I said, "Well look, you can put me in with the engineers if you want to, and I've got nothin' to say about it, but some of my background is medical 'cause I worked in the State Hospital back home and I'd hate to go into engineering where I don't know anything at all about it." So they sent me out to the Mojave Desert and put me into the 67th Medical Regiment of the Third Army. They gave me medical – surgical – training, and I became a combat medic. I went back to the 67th Medical Regiment in 1943 and landed in Oran.

After the battle of Africa started to slow down, and Rommel got tired of running and we got tired of chasing, or something like that, a group of us put in a request to our headquarters to join the 101st Airborne, who were looking for volunteers. Parachuting was always volunteer. There were 14 of us, and we were very close. If one guy got in trouble, then all of us got in trouble!

Well, our request was turned down by our Colonel. But you know how GIs are, they never give up, so we put it back in and after the third attempt we finally won out. So we transferred to England to the 101st and that's where we took our jump training. We did night jump training – we jumped at night. And the first jump that we made there were 300 and some odd casualties, broken legs, broken arms, dislocated shoulders, because you don't see anything at all and you don't know where you're going. And then came the big day when we had the meeting with our officers telling us that this was the last day we would be seeing England. And we left the next day. General Eisenhower came to see us on the landing strips when we departed for a word of encouragement. General Eisenhower was a great man. I knew him before. He was a just man, a very good soldier.

We all loaded into planes, 16 per plane. All together, we were 6,300 in the 101st. Close to a thousand French, 980 I think.

It seems like we landed this morning. Before us there were the pathfinders. They came in first to set up the drop zone lights. I have some buddies that were pathfinders. They took off at midnight and we took off at 1:30. I jumped in and landed on French soil, somewhere between St. Martin de Varreville and Sainte-Mère-Eglise. I made it to the ground, a little hard. We were scattered all over the place. I think out of the two divisions who jumped there were only two or three companies that landed on their d-zones. Everybody else was scattered anywhere from 5 to 35 kms. away. It took some of the paratroopers seven to eight days to get back to their units. The enemy was down there too, so you had to be very careful. We were not far from our d-zone. However, our mission was not to Sainte-Mère-Eglise, our mission was to Carentan. Speaking of the regiments of the 101st, one had to defend Pouppeville, which was on the coast. Another regiment was at St. Côme-du-Mont and also La Barquette. By the end of the 6th of June between both divisions, the 82nd and the 101st, almost all their missions were pretty well accomplished. But there were about 2,760 killed, missing or captured as prisoners.

I was with the 326th Medical Battalion, Company B. We were supposed to head towards Carentan to give medical support to the regiments named to fight over there. We made it. We traveled mostly by night and with the daylight we'd lay low. We had a French kid, a Norman kid, Louis was his name, that led us to our rallying point. We found him when we landed and we asked him how to get there. He said he could take us, showing us how to get there away from the Germans.

It took us about a day to get there. Well, most of a night and part of a day. There was a lot of shooting. There were Germans everywhere. Some of them shot at the aid station but didn't wound anybody. On our way into Carentan we had two or three small bridges over the causeway. On the right-hand side there was what they call the *carré de choux* or "cabbage-patch". It was an immense field of cabbages, and behind that was the German headquarters. We had to go Indian file, and they'd take pot shots at us. Some of the boys got killed. Carentan was very, very difficult. It was well-defended by the Germans. It's sort of in a bucket. We were down below and the Germans were all around and they had their 88's pointed at the town, and they could just about put a shell in your back pocket. Carentan was delivered on the 12th of June.

Our job as medics, of course, was to take the wounded soldiers out and bring them back to the aid station. The doctor would give them the care he could and then we'd evacuate them to the 101st Airborne surgical hospital that was set up in a castle at Heisville. The marshes were all flooded full of water; we picked out roughly about 198 troopers that had drowned due to the marshes. When you jumped you had about 100 lbs. on your back and if you fell over backwards you could forget about getting up. You just couldn't maneuver because there was too much weight. And when they had flooded the marshes or fields, the flooded areas were about a normal person's height. But the causeways where the ocean goes in and out were much deeper, and when you fell in there you just couldn't get out.

In Angoville we took care of some wounded soldiers, American and German, in a church. To us, a soldier is a soldier. Some of them didn't ask to go to the war. We took care of everybody. We took care of our own first, of course, but if there was a German soldier who was really badly injured, we took care of him as fast as we could, too. Anyway, we'd put the wounded on benches and were doing what we could for them. And while we were treating them, a German general and, I suppose, his aides or bodyguards walked in to see what we were doing. He came into the church, walked up front to see what we were doing, and then turned around and walked back out and didn't say a word. We were sure we were going to be picked up as prisoners of war. The battle was going on full blast. But nothing happened to us.

Later, when the 101st had captured some Germans of the 6th Parachute Regiment, one of the prisoners was a doctor. So through our commander, we set him up medically. We gave him a tent and some instruments and said, "Now you can take care of your own people." Believe it or not, I ran into this doctor 18 years later. I was giving a lecture at the Museum of Utah Beach and I saw this person standing in the back. And I thought, "I know I've seen him before but where?" After I'd finished speaking all the lights came on and I walked up the aisle. As if we were automats or robots, we raised hands and said "Carentan" at the same time. Eighteen years later. I invited him for dinner that evening. We send Christmas cards and write, and we try to see each other every year or so in Normandy on the 6th of June.

We didn't stay in Carentan very long. We kept marching, or as we used to say, "we went up the street" toward Paris. Actually, we didn't get into Paris. It was the 4th infantry division that liberated Paris along with General Leclerc. We came up from Normandy but stopped in Versailles in a rest area where we could change our clothes and get a little rest. We were all hoping to get into Paris to liberate it but the General said, "The 101st doesn't have time to go into Paris. We'll go around it and meet on the other side." I guess they figured if they ever let the paratroopers into Paris, they'd never get us out!

So from Versailles we kept on marching. I was up in the front line as a medic, and my job was to go out in the field and pick up the wounded and bring them back to an aid station or a field hospital, depending on how the war ran. We ended our journey through Europe in Berchtesgaden. In the meantime, there was Holland and Bastogne. We took off for Holland on the 17th or 19th of September. After the campaign of Holland we came back to Mourmelon, near

Rheims, to rest and to get new clothes and check our packing. We were supposed to go back to England, but unfortunately we were called to go to Bastogne in the Ardennes. We arrived there on the 19th of December with General McCauliff. The Germans encircled us at 4 o'clock. More than half of us, about 159 of the medical battalion, were later captured by the Germans and taken as prisoners. The weather was very cold. There was a lot of snow and a lot of fog in the beginning. We were running out of ammunition. I know that some of the infantry people only had about three or four bullets in their rifles. We were mainly fed by Belgians, who also gave us some of their sheets so we could wrap ourselves in them and hide ourselves in the snow. We spent a miserable Christmas but we did have turkey and the trimmings.

And thanks to the 3rd Army and General Patton, Colonel Abrams was diverted to come and deliver us – in other words, to make a breach in the ranks of the Germans so that we could be liberated. That's where the famous word "Nuts" comes from. The Germans wanted us to surrender, and General McCauliffe said "Nuts!"

After the War was over, and before I went home, some buddies and I wanted to see Paris because we hadn't seen it before as combat troops coming through. So we put in for a 2-day pass and stayed for six days! And during that time I met the girl who would become my wife.

We were staying at the Magasin Duffaël, a store that had been taken over by the Army. We went to eat at a consolidated mess hall on boulevard St. Denis and took the *métro* coming back. It was loaded with people. I was sitting on one of those small folding seats. She was hanging on to the rails so she wouldn't fall. She didn't look like a French girl because of her hairstyle. She had, I guess you call them, ringlets and was wearing a light, tan hat with a blue ribbon wrapped all round it. She had on a two-piece suit and was carrying a camera. So I said to her, "There are a lot of people, and you're standing and I'm sitting down. Would you like to have my seat?"

She spoke very good English and said, "Thank you very much, but I'm getting off at the next stop." And I said, "That's very funny because I'm getting off at the next stop, too." We got off, and I caught up to her and asked her if she wanted to take some pictures.

She said, "I'd like to, but I don't have any film." It was right after the war, and it was very difficult for people then. "Well, look. I have a lot of film, but I don't have a camera because someone stole it from me yesterday. I'll go up and get it in my room." And she said, "All right. But I'm going to keep on walking." So I ran upstairs at the Magasin Duffaël, grapped a pocketful of film and ran back downstairs and caught up with her. She was going up to Montmartre for a Russian lesson. So we went up the hill and then sat down on a bench overlooking Paris. She started to explain different points of Paris, and we talked and talked. Then she went to her Russian lesson. I waited for her and walked her back to the *métro* afterwards. I never gave her the film. We forgot all about taking pictures.

That was how we met. We got married in Paris in 1947. She was a concert pianist and played classical music. She had 20 students when I married her and three pianos. I worked shifts at the time and told her I couldn't sleep with all the noise. So she sold one piano and kept the other two. And she gave up the students a few at a time.

Roger Lantagne was wounded twice during the war and spent two months in a military hospital. Among other decorations, he was awarded the Purple Heart and the Bronze Star. He remained in the military after the war; of his 31 years of active service, only nine were spent within the United States. He was sent to Korea and volunteered for Vietnam. He was Commander of American Legion Post No. 1 in Paris, and was also active in their service committee, traveling throughout France to help the widows of American war veterans.

Lantagne and Myriam, his French wife of 57 years, have been living in the Paris suburbs since 1973 to be near their two daughters – one a pediatrician, the other a lawyer – and their three grandchildren.

The sergeant

Ted Liska was born into a large Polish family – he was one of ten children – in 1918 in Chicago. Drafted into the army on November 6th, 1941, just one month before Pearl Harbor, he did training in South Carolina, Georgia and Florida before leaving for England and the beaches of France.

We came over from the States in a troop convoy and landed in England in January 1944. Every now and then we would lose a ship but we didn't get caught. Actually, the ship I was on had about seven decks, and we were way down at the bottom in hammocks and so forth, and all the men were sick. All we had was powdered eggs, powdered potatoes, no fresh food. And every now and then they let us go up on top deck and get some exercise, because it seemed like a dungeon down there. There was no fresh air and it smelled. But we knew it wouldn't last long. It only took us five to seven days, from the time we left Camp Kilmer, New Jersey and landed in England at Plymouth or Southampton.

In England I recall that we had an operation which was called Operation Tiger on April the 25th. We were supposed to assault a beach which resembled Utah Beach. It was called Slapton Sands, and it was in Devonshire. We were pretty fortunate. Our regiment landed and we started moving up ahead to take the objective, but, unfortunately, a couple of German U Boats snuck in, and they were able to shell a couple of our boats, and before we knew it there were at least 500 to 700 men killed on a maneuver which was kept top secret till after the war because they didn't want anybody to know what had happened. We had more casualties on this exercise at Slapton Sands than we had in Normandy, the 6th of June, at Utah Beach.

We landed in Normandy at 10:30 in the morning. I was with Company D, 12th Infantry Regiment, 4th Infantry Division. The landing was actually supposed to be the 5th of June, but due to the heavy storm, General Eisenhower postponed it for 24 hours. When we did land on the 6th of June, there were a lot of sick men on our Landing Craft Infantry. I recall before the landing some of the men, the big loudmouths, were bragging: "Well, once we come ashore, we are going to do this and do that." But when we carne ashore on the landing craft, these guys, they were so quiet, and they kept their heads down just like the rest of us.

It's very difficult for people to actually realize what it was like that day. The thousands of men and the shells, the wounded, the dead, the debris, the wrecked tanks, the smoke, the mutilated bodies and everything else. It's very, very difficult. A veteran normally who has seen any combat doesn't brag about what he saw, or what he did. He speaks about others, but very seldom does he speak about what he did.

That day as I was coming over in the landing craft, I said a prayer to myself, "If I come through this alive," I said, "I will never forget the men I leave behind."

They lowered the ramp and we waded ashore. I felt sorry for some of the small men who were loaded down with their equipment, because the water was deep in certain places, but as I was 6 foot 2 and weighed 200 lbs. at the time, the water only came up to my waist. As we approached the shore, I saw a lot of debris, a lot of wreckage, underwater obstacles and so forth. We were pretty fortunate because we landed at the wrong place. We landed two miles from where we were supposed to land. If we'd landed at the right place, there were sea walls there, and we would have had to go over the sea walls, and we might have had a lot of casualties. Where we did land, by mistake, the sand covered the sea walls and we were able to walk across them. And as I recall, the combat engineers did not take all the land mines out of the water, so to the right and left there were land mines still not taken away. An area was taped off with white tape. There was only a small little passage about 10 or 15 yards wide. During all my training as an infantry man, they always used to say, stay 5 to 10 yards between men because one shell would get you all. But here it seemed there were hundreds of men going through a small lane and crossing over the sea wall.

I didn't get more than 500 yards onto the beach and who did I see but Brigadier General Theodore Roosevelt, Jr., who was an Assistant Divisional Commander. He had no steel helmet on, his pants legging was out of his boots, he had a walking stick, and in back of him, he had a first lieutenant with a Thompson submachine gun. And the first words he said were, "Well we landed at the wrong place, but this is where we are going to start."

We only went in about a kilometer or so when we hit water. The Germans had opened up all the dikes and we had to wade in the water for maybe a kilometer or two and we kept on our life preservers. As we went through the water, we were like sitting ducks for the Germans, as they had all their 88's and their pill boxes, and their tanks. They had us all zeroed in, because we could not move fast with the equipment. Once again, I was pretty tall, and every now and then we'd hit a hole. I'd be almost covered up to my head, but for the small men, the water was over their heads.

We were not sure if the Germans were going to use gas. We had our combat fatigues, and over our combat fatigues we had gas-proof clothing, so just in case the Germans did use gas, we were already prepared.

We went about two or three miles inland when we started meeting parachutists from the 82nd and 101st, and they wanted to know what took us so long! As we were going through the fields we saw a lot of wreckage of gliders, as the Germans had put up wooden poles inside the pasture land and a lot of these gliders could not land, and they smashed into these poles. I saw a lot of debris, a lot of bodies and a lot of men lying around.

That night we tried to sleep. I remember telling my men to dig fox holes so that way, if a shell came, we would not get hit. I started digging my fox hole, and I only dug about six inches when I hit cement or rocks. So I said, "Well, I might as well lie down, because if the shell is going to get me, it will get me whether 1 am six feet *under* or six inches *above* ground."

I saw many of my buddies get wounded and killed in the first couple of days of the campaign. We fought from Sainte Mère-Eglise into Cherbourg, which we took June 25th, 1944. Actually, Cherbourg was our main objective because the Americans needed the port so we could bring in all our supplies. We were supposed to take it in 10 days but it was actually almost two weeks before we entered Cherbourg. One of the things I do remember is the town of Montebourg. We went into Montebourg the 10th of June, the Germans pushed us out the 11th, we went in again the 12th of June, the Germans pushed us out the 13th, and finally we went in the 14th of June, and then from Montebourg we went into Valognes, and on our way to Cherbourg.

And I also recall the Battle of St. Lô when it seemed like thousands of planes were overhead, and that's what they call the breakthrough, where General Patton started his drive into Paris and going towards Belgium. At that time American planes dropped a couple of smoke bombs, and they killed and wounded many Americans by air, because they dropped their smoke bombs, and due to the wind they dropped the bombs too close.

In the first 60 days of combat four of the men in our unit were killed, and there were about 15 wounded. I remember when 1 was training with my men, most of them were a little smaller than me. And they would always say, "Boy, Sarge, you stick out like a big GMC truck. We're gonna stay behind you, and we won't get hit.". Well here I was, leading my men, and some of my men to my right and left did get wounded or killed.

And I also recall when I was wounded, the 10th of August, at the Battle of Mortain. I was wounded in the right thigh, by shrapnel. I was pretty fortunate because I was big and muscled. I was behind a hedge row, and when I got up, I called right away for an aid man. An aid man came, and he gave me morphine and put some sulfa powder over my wound. He said, "Sarge, we're going to have to evacuate you; we're going to get a stretcher and take you back." I said, "No, you don't have to get a stretcher. I can walk back." I stood up, and I fell down in cow manure because I couldn't stand. So the first lieutenant and his radio man, plus two aid men, took me back. We only went maybe a half mile, and we were caught in a shell barrage. The four men took cover and laid me down flat. Shrapnel hit the lieutenant and his radio operator, but nothing happened to me while I was out in the open. Instead of being one casualty going back, there were three of us! Then I went to Cherbourg. They evacuated me by boat, and 1 stayed in a hospital in Birmingham, England for 89 days.

And because I was in the hospital, I missed the liberation of Paris on the 25th of August, 1944. Paris was liberated by the 12th Infantry Regiment, 4th Infantry Division, the unit I was with when we landed on D-Day. They even had a mass at Nôtre Dame Cathedral with the chaplain from our 12th Regiment, Chaplain Fries.

Released from the hospital in December 1944, Liska returned to France and served at Compiègne, training men from other branches of the service for the infantry. From late 1945 through 1946, he was a First Sergeant in the Military Police in Paris. In June 1946, he made his first pilgrimage to Normandy, thus fulfilling the promise he made to the men he left behind on Utah Beach. Except for 1951 and 1965, when he was serving in Korea and Vietnam, he has returned every June since then, at his own expense, to pay homage to those buried at the St. Laurent Cemetery.

From 1946 to 1949 Sergeant Liska was assigned as an Honor Guard at the Sainte-Mère-Eglise cemetery, where he comforted American families by sharing with them his vivid recollections. He was chosen to serve as a French interpreter for Dwight D. Eisenhower in 1951 and 1963, when the former President toured the Normandy area. Liska retired from the U.S. Army in 1973 after 33 years of service. He has been awarded the Croix de Guerre, *the Bronze Star, the Combat Infantry Badge, the Vietnamese Medal of Honor and the Vietnamese Gallantry Cross. He is an honorary citizen of Sainte-Marie-du-Mont, Utah Beach and Sainte-Mère-Eglise.*

After his retirement from the military, Liska and his French wife, Raymonde, resided in Belgium, moving to Paris in 1988. He is presently employed in the Postal Unit of the American Embassy. The Liskas have two sons, both of whom are career officers in the U.S. Air Force.

The cook

In 1941 an 18-year-old Massachusetts boy was drafted into the army. He became a cook and was sent to England and France. This is his story.

I was drafted in '41. I went down for basic training at Fort McClellan in Alabama. That's where you do one foot forward, and two back, on that red dirt of Alabama. After that we were shipped off and we landed in a port called Gairloch in Scotland. We were taken down by train to a little place in England called Yeovil, in Somerset County. A little town, beautiful place, like a picture post-card.

I don't remember when I landed in France. I think it was five or six days after D-Day. In any case, I was in France before the Battle of St. Lô. I landed on Utah Beach. I don't remember the name of the landing craft. We were packed up like beasts, though. They kept prodding us to move up. We didn't have a chance to look around and ask questions. It seemed like hours coming across.

One thing we noticed all around us when we landed were the bar-rage balloons put up on the beachheads to keep the Germans from coming down and scraping us. I think they were packed in with helium. They'd blow the balloons up and then float them with cables. They were to keep the Germans from coming in straight at us. The Germans could drop something over that, but they couldn't come in low. We had the balloons in England, too, around our base camp in that little town of Yeovil.

We landed, and after we hit the beach, they hiked us inland. It was more hectic than anything else. Everything went so fast. They just told us to keep moving in. Then we were in this apple orchard and they told us to dig holes – or slit trenches, as we called them then – where we had to sleep.

We were bombed one night next to this big farmhouse. In this farmhouse there was a courtyard with pavement. And with the explosion, not necessarily close by – it could have been in the fields next to us – but the bombing caused the windows to snap out and break. It was an incident you remember. Falling down on the courtyard, a windowpane dropping down, it's just like any glass that you break, and it makes noise. Well, that was our first baptism of fire, if you wish. And we were scared stiff, I mean we were scared stiff. Some of our N.C.O.s were battle-trained already because they had fought in other areas before. They just laughed at us when we told them we'd got scared the night before because of the glass. It was a stupid incident but, as I say, it was the real first battle fright we had. And we were scared. We thought, "What the hell is going to come next?" And these officers said, "If you think that's something, that's absolutely nothing. When you go further, you're going to get baptized by a heck of a lot worse than that."

Another night we were all in these little slit trenches, in this apple orchard, and the German planes came over and they bombed us. Why did they bomb *us?* First of all, there was a concentration of us troops, there. Number Two, how did they know we were there? Something stupid. One or more of us had left our mess kits out, and the mess kits at night, from what we were told, glared. And from a plane you could certainly see an aluminium mess kit! That's why we were told to darken our mess kits. If somebody didn't, they could see that from above and they knew there was a concentration of troops down there. And that's how they bombed us.

Our officers told us to keep that incident as a lesson, that when we were told to do something, we were told to do so for a reason. We'd asked, "What the hell? Why darken our mess kits?" We thought they were crazy. But when you see something like that happen, then it dawns on you. It makes an impression.

Anyway, we were waiting outside St. Lô to be called in. I was anti-tank crew, and I came in as a replacement as an antitank guy. I had an M.O.S. number but was also a cook for the army. They needed cooks in front-line kitchens, and they looked me up because I had an M.O.S. number. They found me and asked me if I wanted to go into a field kitchen. And I told them yes, I'd go along with them.

The field kitchen was just a few miles behind the lines because the troops came in from the lines to eat hot chow. We had these gas ranges that we used to pump up. We worked out in the cold and the rain and whatnot. I remember one day it was raining like hell and we still worked out there. And the troops would come inside with their mess kits. It was like a regular kitchen, but outside under tents. There were about 12 of us working there. It was hard work. I guess we were outside St. Lô about a week.

When we moved right after the Battle of St. Lô, with all the scrapings and the bombings of the area there, the dust in the air was so thick you could almost cut it with a knife. The Americans dropped smoke bombs to get the Germans out of the trenches they'd built all around the city. And something else. There was the red-ball highway and the yellow-ball highway. They were special routes that were taken over by the Allies and were strictly for military use.

I went back to the replacement depot. We were waiting there to see where we were going to be called in to. One day the sergeant who was in charge there had me called into the office and he told me to pack up. I asked him where I was heading for. Everything went by an APO number. And so he said, "You're going to APO number so forth." I wanted to know where it was. But he said "Don't worry about it. Just pack up and go." So I said, "Can't I stay here a few more days?" And he said, "Don't be stupid. If you only knew where you were going. So many people would love to go where you're going." So I said, "Regardless. I still want to stay here a few more days." That was because I'd made some friends in the area. Finally, word got out that particular APO number was Paris. Paris had just been liberated, and they wanted to open up mess halls there. So they packed us up and we moved that night by truck, blinking lights out front there.

We came to the city, and we stopped in front of a big building in Paris in the 18th *arrondissement* called Magasin Duffaël. That was a central gathering point. That's where the army first opened up some offices. I guess the Germans were there before we arrived. The Germans pulled out and we pulled in. They had bunk beds upstairs for officers and troops. It was used for a long time afterwards.

I got hooked onto one of the biggest mess halls, a transit mess. Transit Mess No.5, in Paris, at Strasbourg-St. Denis. At that time it was called Hotel Marguerite. It was a former German restaurant. As soon as Paris was liberated, we came in and we took over this place that the Germans had just moved out of. I worked there from a few weeks after the Liberation right to the end of '46. I know it was then because right at the beginning of '47 I pulled out on discharge. I was a mess sergeant, one of the mess sergeants who was running that mess hall, and was attached to the Seine Area Command.

I remember the climate that winter. I've never seen as much snow as there was at that time, and you can check with the French people about that. The electricity was cut off. It was at 10:30 at night. Everything was highly rationed. The French women wore wooden shoes, which would clatter when they walked down the street. That was because leather was so scarce.

The mess hall was a transit mess. The difference between a transit mess and a stationary mess is that in a transit mess the troops are in transit; they keep coming and going to the front, coming back from the lines. And, in Paris, there were a number of transit messes, including some in railway stations, where the troops ate and boarded these trains that kept going further north, into Germany and Belgium. The mess hall where I was attached, N° 5, was the second biggest mess hall. I can remember distinctly a figure from those days, during the Battle of Bastogne, about the troops that came in from the ports of France through Paris and went up by truck, train or otherwise and ate in my mess hall. I remember working a 24-hour period, round the clock, and feeding 25,000 troops! And that was in a small place. It was the second biggest mess hall, but still it was small compared to some army mess halls. That was because it was during the Battle of Bastogne, and there were troops everywhere.

The food was mostly imported food that carne in from the States. Everything was in cans, dehydrated or dried foods. We did have, however, meats, beef carcasses, that came in from Argentina. And in my mess hall I had German prisoners of war working for me. I had a whole team. I had butchers, bakers, but no candlestick makers! Seriously, though, I did have bakers, and the butchers used to cut up the meat, and other people used to make salads and whatnot from anything we could lay our hands on. Most of these people worked in mess halls in the German army. We asked for them. When we needed someone to work in the kitchen to do a special job we used to call the Prisoner of War camp and they'd send us as many as we needed. These prisoners were hauled out every night. Trucks, American trucks, came to my mess hall, picked up the prisoners, and they used to haul them to a camp outside the city, I don't know where. I just know they'd take them there every night and then bring them back to me.

We had steam tables. The soldiers served themselves on dishes and plastic trays. The prisoners, who were Germans and even some French, by the way, picked up the dishes.

The troops came in either from the States, England or other parts of France, when they were needed. They'd come through Paris, and the last meal they had before they went up north to join the lines was at my place, which was a transit place. All of them asked me if I had heard the stories of the lines, the atrocities. They were scared of the atrocities. Those were the questions they asked, how the Germans treated you if you became a prisoner. I told them, from what I had heard, as I treat my German personnel here. I said in Europe, the Germans in principle, in principle I said, treated the prisoners half-way decent. They went by the Geneva Convention mules, whereas the Japanese didn't.

I worked pretty hard. But we did have a number of days off throughout the course of the year when we could take a rest. I drove out of the city and visited the countryside, Fontainebleau, Versailles, went back to Rouen, places like that. The real bombs and damage were done deep out in the countryside. There were places that were blasted, yes, but very little war damage. I took my jeep, which was attached to the mess hall. Sometimes I took friends with me.

I would rather remain anonymous. I'm no hero. My brother was banged up during the war. Both of my brothers, for that matter. And the one brother has been suffering for 50 years, and they're probably going to have to amputate his leg after all this time. I saw my best buddies drop dead and get slaughtered and whatnot there. When I saw all that, I felt I did so little compared to them. I didn't even pick up the medals I was supposed to receive. What I did I did because either I had to do it or I went along with the others. They say, "The Man Upstairs protected me." That's all. But when you see your own buddies there...

I have a good story about "The Man Upstairs." We had a religious ceremony in an apple orchard in Normandy. Our chaplain – he happened to be a Catholic chaplain – came out to give a service in the field there. He had one of those portable altars. All the people who went there weren't only Catholics, though. The Chaplain talked to us and he said, "Hey, listen fellows. You're here today and I'm talking to you. Some of you people won't hear me anymore. Listen carefully. When you're in the lines and a shell bursts, and it comes down close to you and it chops off your buddy's head in the same trench with you or otherwise close-by, what are the first words you say?" Then he said, and he was a smart one, "You say, 'Oh, my God!'" This is natural. I mean when nowadays there's an accident out in the street, what do people say? So the chaplain said, "At that time why do you say 'Oh, my God'"? Why don't you say, 'Oh, my mother!' or 'Oh, my sister!' or something else? Since you say 'Oh my God' at that time, say it now. So kneel and pray." That's a good story, isn't it?

The mess sergeant asked to be discharged in Paris in the early part of 1947. In order to stay abroad, however, he needed a passport. After much negotiation, he persuaded the American Embassy to issue him one. He believes he was the first American in Paris to be issued a U.S. passport after the war. He has lived in Paris ever since his discharge, except for six years in the mid-1950s, when he helped supervise the construction of four U.S. air bases in North Africa. After holding a number of different jobs and running his own business, he retired in 1989. His second wife is French, and he has three dual-national children and one grandchild.

When asked why he has stayed in France all these years, he says: "Life was really wonderful in Paris after the war. Americans were regarded as heroes. I've always shunned the idea of being a hero, but you were treated a lot better, shall we say. Well, there was that, and then I started to go to school on the GI Bill. I went to the Cordon Bleu and got a cooking diploma there. I also went to the Alliance Française and the Ecole Berlitz to learn French. And then, like everything else, you fall into the groove. For instance, eating French bread. We got such a liking for eating the French baguette. *Or sitting at a café on the Champs-Elysées. You could order a cup of coffee and stay all afternoon. We didn't have much money, so a bunch of us would sit down there and gab all afternoon on a cup of coffee. They didn't rush us and tell us they had to get ready for the next customer and we had to get out. Or we'd go for a cup of coffee and listen to the music. When the war ended, it was unbelievable the number of cafés that had little orchestras. So many little things like that. 'Wine, women and song' was our motto. We met girls and went out. We made friends, American and French, at the Legion and other places. So with all that put together, Paris got to you."*

The french resistant

Born in 1924 in a little village near Neufchâtel in Normandy, Maurice Quillien was fifteen and still a student at secondary school when the war broke out in 1939. Ordered to evacuate by British military authorities, the Quilliens spent some time with family in Brittany. Upon their return in July 1940, they found their home destroyed by German bombs and the town of Neufchâtel (pop. 3,500-4,000) in ruins.

Quillien returned to school but began work as an employee-secretary of a farm machinery company the day after he received his diploma in July 1941. The owners of the company were two childhood friends who had lost their parents in the bombings. Very patriotic, they enlisted Quillien's help in the resistance movements that were getting under way.

The firm where I worked was both a repair shop for farm machinery and a sawmill. It was continuously being requisitioned by the German army, as there were many sites in the sector for the assembling, stocking and launching of V-1s.

During the German occupation, there was a 9 p.m. curfew, so that people who finished work day late had to carry what they called an *Ausweis*. This was a permit that allowed you to be in the streets during the curfew, which, I think, was from 9 p.m. to 6 a.m. The German patrols would, of course, stop you if they saw you out during that time. If you had an *Ausweis,* you'd show it to them. If you didn't have one, you made a fast getaway.

In our area, we were privileged because we lived on farms. In cities like Rouen or Paris, people had it much tougher. That's why we used to see a lot of Parisians coming out to stock up on food. They came by train every day of the week with empty suitcases and returned with them full at about 4:30 p.m. On their way back, many got off before Paris, and a friend with a bike and trailer came to get what they had in the suitcases. The Germans would say, half in German, half in French: *Franzose, groß filous....* You French are big rogues. *Großfilous* was an expression the Germans used a lot at the time.

The people who came were, on the whole, regular customers. They dealt with one or two farms where they had regular relations, and so many eggs and *kilos* of meat or butter – which they'd buy way above the market price – were reserved for them each week. It was a time of black-market trading, and there were people who made a living just from that. Some were involved in very lucrative trafficking. Not everyone, of course.

On September 23rd, 1943 – about a year before the liberation of Neufchâtel – my bosses, Serge and René Flambard, and I got involved in what you might call the "search and rescue" of allied airmen of the U.S. Air Force and the Royal Air Force. It all began then. After this, I got in touch with the head of the local Resistance group. My parents were also brought in, as I was single and still lived at home. I would bring back airmen, and they never refused to take them in.

It was on that day that we came to the aid of William McGonigle. A schoolmate of mine working for the highways department had discovered a man in uniform hiding behind a haystack and told Serge and Réné about it. He said he thought he was an American or English airman but he didn't know which because at the time we didn't recognize the color of the uniforms.

Serge and René sent me out to Bouelles, on the Neufchâtel-Forges-les-Eaux road, on the company's motorcycle. It was really unusual for us to use the *moto* at the time because it was very difficult to get gas, so we didn't waste it. Well, I took the *moto* and found the haystack and the man hiding there. In my broken English I asked him if was British. He made me understand that he was American and that he'd been shot down from a Marauder. We didn't want to do anything against their will, so I asked him if he wanted to be made a prisoner by the Germans or wanted us to hide him. He chose the second option.

I hid him in a shepherd's hut and told him to stay there until I came back. That evening I drove out there on the motorcycle, followed by Serge and René in the car, a Citroën front-wheel drive. After checking out the area to see nobody was there, I signaled to Serge and Réne and we got McGonigle into the car. They drove him to my parents' house, and I followed by motorcycle.

My parents were warned about and approved of what we were doing. But they lived in the courtyard of the sawmill where the logs were stocked. Every day Germans or foremen of the work on the V-1s came by. So it was decided that McGonigle should be sent to another place, to the house of the town tax-collector. From there, thanks to Roger Cressin, the town clerk, he was sent to Paris and who knows where afterwards. We never knew what happened to him or his fellow crew members, and we never found his plane. Even after the war and despite the request I made to the U.S. Air Force, I wasn't able to obtain any more information.

We started helping U.S. Air Force and R.A.F. airmen. That was how my Resistance activities began. One important thing we had to do was to get them identity papers. Because for the Germans, there was only one thing that counted and that was justification of one's identity. "Papers?" (with a German accent) was always the first question they asked us. Town clerks like Roger Cressin would make them false identity cards.

Just as important was to provide the men with civilian clothes. That was often comical because we'd get civilian clothes for an average-sized guy and he'd turn out to be very tall! Some of them ended up with trousers and sleeves that were much too short.

Even though under the occupation, all French people who had radios, which we called T.S.F., or "wireless", had to turn them in at the *Mairie*[1], my parents had a receiver. People who'd had two radio sets only turned one in. And handymen like Serge Flambard made crystal sets. But only the heads of Resistance departments or groups had transmitters. That was the difference.

---

(1) This law applied to the six administrative districts in north western France closest to England.

We were very lucky because during all the period before the liberation of Neufchâtel by Canadian troops on September 1st, 1944, we were never denounced, nor was our house searched by the *Feld Gendarmerie* – the German police – or the French police working for the Germans.

Yes, we were very lucky and we realized it. We realize it even more now that we know about the difficulties that some people had. At the time we didn't know about the extermination camps that everybody knows about now. It was only after the end of the war in May 1945 that we heard on the radio that allied troops – Soviet, English and American – had liberated prisoners from camps that were not internment camps but extermination camps. Auschwitz, Buchenwald and many others.

French families with members who'd been deported didn't know what happened to them when they were sent to Germany. It was the same thing for POWs and shot-down airmen, who were, in a sense, lucky not to be killed but unlucky to be found by the German police and sent off to prison camps.

Our "search and rescue" of airmen meant we risked, if we were found, being sent to work camps. We thought they were work camps, whereas they were, in fact, extermination camps. My parents would also have been deported.

I don't know how many of us there were in the network. You knew those close to you; one of these knew another, who knew others. But you had to compartmentalize to avoid giving names of other members of a network during possible interrogations. Even though we didn't know about the existence of extermination camps, we did know that they tortured people during interrogations.

At the end of June 1944 we hid another American at our house: Gus Bubenzer. His plane, an A 20 Havoc, had been shot down, and he'd jumped and fallen near the national Neufchâtel-Aumale-Amiens highway. We were a rather well-structured network by that time. Gus was staying with some farmers, Monsieur and Madame Corroyer, on an isolated farm near a forest. But there were neighbors or farm employees who were asking questions, such as: "What's that guy doing there? It isn't normal to see a 20-year old boy not working."

As people were talking, the farmer asked Roger Cressin to find another hiding place. So Roger Cressin came to see me at home, saying there was another airman somewhere, he didn't know where, and it would be a good idea to hide him because there was a certain risk of denunciation. Only when my parents said that yes, they would take him did he say where he was. I went off with two bicycles, one for me and the other for Gus. I arrived at Marcel Corroyer's to take delivery. He'd been warned by Roger Cressin. A hidden airman was never given over to just anyone. Gus didn't know how to ride a bike very well, but that day he really proved himself. We rode down from the farm where he was to Neufchâtel and on to my parents'. That's how Gus came to us.

When we got to the main intersection of Neufchâtel, a German in uniform came up to me. He'd been in Neufchâtel for several months and knew a lot of local inhabitants. He recognized me, especially because he used to come to the firm where I was working. And he asked me, with his German accent, "Ça va?"– everything okay? Gus, seeing me speaking with the German, became frightened. He thought we'd been caught and made a U-turn. So when I was ready to start off again, Gus wasn't there anymore. But I found him, and we went on to my parents' house.

Gus stayed with us from the end of June until September 1st, when Neufchâtel was liberated. My brother shared his bed with Gus, the American. And Alan Nicol, an Englishman with the R.A.F. who'd been shot down from a Lancaster at Haudricourt, slept with me. This allowed for a certain sense of security, since the bedrooms were on the ground floor and therefore easily accessible for people like the Germans, who would knock on the windows at night to ask for something. That's why it was very important not to put the American and the Englishman together They would have had trouble answering the Germans' questions. In such cases, my brother or I would immediately speak up and give the answer.

Gus was very accommodating, calm, posed and reflective. All of the airmen were accommodating, by the way. Looking back with age, I'm convinced that in their various briefings they'd been taught to find protection among the French population rather than to be made prisoners by the Germans. But don't forget, these French people thus incurred great risks, and I'm sure the airmen realized this.

They knew they were indebted to us and that's why they were very disciplined and respected the instructions we gave them.

The airmen spent most of their time with my mother and my brother, who, at that time, was still at school. They tried to help in household chores. As the only means we had of heating and cooking was a wood stove, they sawed wood and chopped kindling for us. We raised rabbits because it was very difficult to get meat, so grass had to be found on the plains and in the fields. They tried to make themselves useful by doing all these tasks. But when they were away from our house, they had to stay on their own. If someone came towards them, they would move away to avoid making conversation. They couldn't always make people believe they were deaf and dumb.

I could talk about the bombings. There was a distinction: night bombings were done by the Royal Air Force and day bombings by the U.S. Air Force. The bombers all came from British airfields. During the occupation, the bombings were mostly directed against German structures such as those built for the V-1s. We were bombed during the day and at night...

Conditions were rather difficult. First of all, the rather frequent machine-gunning of locomotives came without warning. We'd be near the station – trains were used much more then than now – and the hedgehopping American or British fighters would go: "ra-ta-ta-ta". Sometimes they succeeded in getting the locomotive, sometimes they didn't. Right away, German guns, usually a quadruple battery of pom-pom cannon at each end of the train, retaliated.

When the planes hedgehopped, the firing of anti-tank artillery passed just above our heads, too. What a bang it made! Until recently there used to be a building near here where you could still see shell shots in its wooden walls.

I remember D-day. I was with my parents and Serge Flambard in St. Sens on June 4, 1944 for the first communion of his young sister-in-law. Even during the war, it was inconceivable, of course, for a family ceremony, such as a communion, baptism, or wedding, to last less than two days! We were therefore still going strong at dawn on June 6th. The activity we heard overhead had a different sort of sound. In the preceding weeks and months, we'd heard thousands, hundreds of thousands, of planes, but they were at a higher altitude, and the humming lasted for hours. This was different. The planes flew lower, abnormally and unusually so. On the T.S.F. we heard: "*Français, Françaises*, the allied landing is taking place." So, we knew. But we didn't know about it beforehand. Only those who were in contact with the higher circles of the Resistance knew what the message[1] meant.

In July, because of the bombings of Neufchâtel and the risks facing our airmen, we thought it best to move. We also wanted to avoid being noticed by our neighbors. So we went to live at the Adamses' farm in Menonval for two weeks. After that, we went to live in a very rustic house in Broche-Menonval. There were also several other families at the Adamses' place who had taken in airmen, including three Englishmen – Gardner, Wilkinson and Bishop – and two Americans, Henry Hodulik and Gene Young.

Henry Hodulik had jumped from a Marauder and found himself near the Londinières-Neufchâtel road, in the hamlet of Neuville, which was part of Bailleul-Neuville. Intuitive, subtle, lively, he realized right away there was a forest nearby, so he ran up a slope and hid there. I had a friend, André Vasselin, a farmer at the time, who saw the parachute come down and then somebody running towards the woods. The Germans were looking around elsewhere, so my friend ran over there.

Although my friend didn't speak English and Henry didn't speak French, they somehow seemed to understand each other. My friend told him he'd be back at 10 o'clock at night to get him and that in the meantime someone would bring him some bread, a bottle of cider and a piece of bacon. But when my friend came back to get him, Henry was gone. Either he didn't understand, or if he did, he got impatient, which wouldn't surprise me at all because he was a live wire.

Henry wandered about in the countryside and was found the next morning. He'd walked all night and arrived at about 6 or 6:30 in the morning at the little railway station of Mesnières-en-Braye. The station master at the time, Monsieur Frelais, asked him: "What are you doing here?" And he answered: "I'm American." Fortunately, he fell

---

(1) "les sanglots longs des violons..."

on someone sympathetic and comprehensive who understood he had to hide Henry, because he was still in uniform! Incredible as it may seem, except for Vasselin, he hadn't run into anyone else. So Frelais made him come in and gave him some civilian clothes. Then he contacted the network, in other words the Flambard brothers, and that's how Henry got to the Adamses' farm, where the photo was taken with five other airmen.

Henry stayed with Gene Young, his crewman, on the Adamses' farm until the liberation of Neufchâtel. Gene was young and energetic but didn't fly off the handle as easily as Henry, who was quite highly strung. I don't really remember how Gene got to the Adamses'. As for Hodulik's story, I'm sure that's what happened.

I remember an incident with Henry. It was after the allied landings. He was only 21 and very spontaneous and dynamic. A bomb – the one that destroyed the house of the gatekeeper – fell about 100 meters from us. It really made a din. Henry, spontaneous as he was, leapt up and shouted, "But the allies are crazy. Neufchâtel isn't a military objective." He was right, it wasn't a military objective. He saw what it was like being on the receiving end. If we hadn't kept him back, he was ready to leave, to try and cross the line and tell the allied troops: "You're crazy! You've bombed Neufchâtel. Where's the military objective?" We were able to calm him down, and he stayed.

There's another anecdote about something I didn't experience personally because I had to work on a farm in order to feed us all. Because I "neglected" to register with the German labor "recruiters", I didn't have a ration card, and, obviously, there were no ration tickets for people in hiding like Gus and Alan Nichol. For after all, we didn't just give them lodging, we had to feed them, too. And they were twenty and thirty year olds! That's why I was working on a farm.

So I wasn't there on August 31, 1944, on the eve of the liberation of Neufchâtel, when three Germans beating a retreat stopped at my parents' house, which only had a ground floor. My father and I weren't there, but my mother was with Gus and Alan Nichol. A German asked Alan for a light for his cigarette. My mother stepped right in and said, "Excuse me, Sir. He's deaf and dumb. He can neither hear nor speak." "Oh, *groß malheur*" – what ill luck. Then my mother took a box of matches and said, "Help yourself."

As I said, the Germans were beating a retreat. It was just after "the Falaise pocket" breakthrough. Well, my mother convinced them to stop their journey there, and with their approval she locked them up in the part of the basement where we kept the cheese. "*La guerre kaput, groß malheur*" – the war's over, what ill luck. My mother actually convinced them and they let themselves be locked up. She gave them some milk, bread, butter and meat and then turned them over to the liberating troops, the Canadians, the next day.

So the next day the Canadians arrived and opened the basement door. The Germans saw the khaki uniforms and Gus and Alan with my mother. And the German who spoke a little French, the one who had asked for a cigarette the day before, heard Alan and Gus speaking and said to my mother, "Madame, yesterday Monsieur no speak, today speak." And my mother replied, "Ah, yes, Monsieur. Yesterday was yesterday, and today is today." That was an incident that marked the end of Gus and Alan's stay with us.

After the war, Quillien wasn't mobilized, but he enlisted, as other Resistants did, in the battalions that were being constituted. He was in the 5th Battalion in Rouen. When it was dissolved, he went to Tunis to back up the 4th Regiment of Zouaves until June 1946. After being discharged from the army, he became a sales representative. He has been retired since August 1984.

Married since 1949, Quillien is the father of a daughter, Nelly. Quillien's mother, who died in 1989, was named President of the Local Liberation Committee of Neufchâtel from 1944 to 1946.

Quillien is president of the 5th Battalion Normandy Veterans Association and Honorary President of the Franco-British Sister Cities Association of Neufchâtel. He is on the board of another veterans association and is a member of an association for reserve non-commissioned officers. He is also a member of the Friends of the Order of Merit Association.

He received the American Medal of Freedom, the highest civilian distinction given by the U.S. government, from General Eisenhower in 1945. Later, he was given a Certificate of Gratitude signed by the President of the United States, Dwight Eisenhower. He has received the Gold Medal from the American Legion and the Knight's Cross from the Pologna Restituta (the Polish government exiled in London). He also has two Belgian distinctions: the Order of Merit and Chevalier of the Belgian Cross. He was recently named Chevalier of the French National Order of Merit.

Of the eight allied airmen Quillien helped, four are still alive. Several of them return periodically to France to visit the family that aided them.

The radio signalman

Born in Paris, France, in 1921, of an American father and a French mother, Guy Dunham had just finished high school at the Lycée Henri IV, and was on his way to the University of Virginia, when the War broke out. Paris was his home. He had grown up there, gone to French schools and had dual-citizenship at the time. His parents, exporters of fine linens and lace, had met during World War I. In 1919, Dunham's father, a doughboy, had returned to Dijon to marry his mother and to settle permanently in France. With the coming of World War II, however, they were forced to pull up stakes and leave the country, as 90% of their business was with the United States.

My father drove an ambulance in Paris for a short while at the beginning of the War, and then my parents left for New York. There were plenty of candidates to drive ambulances who were much more competent than my father was. I think he once forgot to check the water, and it was rather disastrous.

I entered the American Army at the end of November 1942. After basic training, I was assigned to the 445th Anti-aircraft Battalion. We were shipped to England from Fort Hamilton in February of 1944. We went across on the *Pasteur*, a former French liner taken over by the Canadian Royal Navy shortly after France fell. Since the *Pasteur* was a very fast ship, we crossed by ourselves and were not in a convoy. We had air cover all along the American and Canadian coasts and again once we got a day out of Ireland. It was quite an exciting crossing because, apparently, we picked up a submarine on our radar, so we had to take a detour and go north. The whole trip took seven days and the sea was very rough; we rolled a lot, and a great many people were sick. Some people never left their bunks. They just stayed there throughout the trip and didn't eat.

We landed in Liverpool, which, as often happened, was being bombed that day by the Luftwaffe. We trained in Wales and then spent three or four months in Devonshire. We were there at the time of the landings in Normandy. I remember very well because I was on guard duty that night and I heard rumbles in the distance and the next day we discovered the landings had taken place. We knew they were about to take place because we had been given maps which were to be opened when we got on the Continent. We didn't know when we would go. We knew it would be to France but we didn't know exactly where.

We landed on the 9th of July 1944 at Omaha Beach. We left immediately by truck and went on to Carentan, which I remember because I was awakened as Carentan was under German shellfire. From Carentan we went to St. Sauveur-le-Vicomte in the Cotentin, and there we regrouped and moved on to the division to which we were attached until the end of the fighting in Europe, and this was the 8th Infantry Division. The 8th Infantry Division had been posted in and trained in Ulster in Northern Ireland. We joined up with them on the 10th, I'd say, and we moved our command post, and our various batteries, around La Haye-du-Puits, which the GI's called "La Hay du Poots". It had been fought over between the Americans and the Germans and had been taken and retaken. I myself was a P.F.C. at the time and had been given a hand-powered radio with which I was supposed to give so-called flash signals announcing any German aircraft or even any enemy ground action.

So as soon as we were in position, this was a mile or two miles in front of La Haye-du-Puits, we were shelled because divisional artilleries wee in the next field. We were caught in counter battery fire, and that was the first time I was under close shelling. Thank God we had all properly dug our fox holes! That was when we realized how useful the fox holes were. I picked up a piece of shell that had narrowly missed my bottom by about 10 centimeters. It was still very hot and I'm sure would have caused the kind of injury that makes people titter.

I was in that very spot when the bombing of the city of St. Lô took place. St. Lô, the capital of the department of the Manche, on the Cotentin peninsula, was shelled because it was an important network. The story goes that most of the German army had already moved out, but you always hear that sort of thing *post facto*. In any case, it was a remarkable and awesome sight to see all these American bombers flying in magnificent and majestic formations, and once in a while one would simply just blow up when hit by German anti-aircraft. This was also around the time when, unfortunately, some of the bombing of the German lines and Saint-Lô was erroneously made on our own lines. Probably nothing would have been heard of it, except that General McNair, commander of all the training camps in America, was on an inspection tour at the wrong time and was killed by his own side.

Two or three days after this, the big push started. We went across the Lessay-St. Lô road and moved on by very dusty roads on the tail of the Germans, who were by now fleeing south. At that time we were under the Third Army. I had the honor of seeing General Patton in his jeep and shining helmet and side pistols and so on, looking just like you've seen him in all his pictures. We were scraped a couple of times by the Luftwaffe, but on the whole the Germans had few planes. They did have a plane, though, which we called "Bedtime Charlie" that came every night looking for our position. In the daytime the Luftwaffe planes were few and far between, but very often they flew very low, and the Cotentin was hedgerow country, so actually you barely had time to shoot a few rounds.

We went to the various places that had been liberated. The French people were full of joy and especially appreciated our cigarettes and candy, and, in the beginning at least, we were extremely generous with the local population. Some of the other soldiers knew a bit of French, but I was the only one who knew Normandy, since I'd spent part of my childhood there. So one of my jobs was to trade some of our rations for a little of the local brew, an applejack called *Calavados*. Later, in Brittany, I would trade them for fresh vegetables and eggs.

From Coutances, we went down to Avranches and saw the havoc on some of the roads. Havoc which had been wrought by the P47s, I think it was mostly P47s, of the American air force scraping German convoys. It was quite a sight. The Army engineers had to clear German vehicles, dead horses and whatever you want from the road, and with the heat and so on, there was rather a pungent smell. (...)

From Normandy, Dunham went on with the 445th Anti-Aircraft Battalion into Brittany, then to Luxembourg, Germany, Belgium and Holland. Shipped back to the U.S. from Antwerp on a Liberty Ship that took 17 days to cross the Atlantic, he was discharged at Fort Dix in December 1945. His homecoming was a sad one: his widowed mother (his father had died of a heart attack three weeks after he arrived in England) was critically ill; and his brother had been injured during training as a combat engineer.

Dunham attended Fordham University on the G.I. Bill as a graduate student and then Columbia University Law School, from which he graduated in June 1949. He has been practicing law in Paris since 1955 and is a member of the New York Bar, the Washington D.C. Bar and the Paris Bar. His wife is English, and they have two sons, both dual nationals. He is Vice President of the Mona Bismarck Foundation and is on the Board of the American Library of Paris.

The news broadcaster

As the father of an infant son and an instructor of French in a government program in New York City for Navy cadets, there was little likelihood that Sim Copans, who was born in 1912, would have been mobilized. But in late 1943 when a friend in the Office of War Information told him they were looking for bilingual people to go to England and France to do radio work, he talked it over with his French wife and decided that he should sign up. Both he and Lucienne wanted their children to be able to say that their father had somehow participated in the war. After radio training in the U.S. and a stint with ABSIE (American Broadcasting System in Europe) in England, he volunteered to go off for military training and be part of the landing operation of the First Army.

For two or three weeks, we were given a very painful introduction in uniform to carrying heavy bags on our backs. We walked ten miles with these darned things, dug trenches, put up tents, slept outside. The army could do miracles in a short time to us civilians who had no previous army experience!

We were moved more than once. What I remember about that period in the English countryside was being impressed by the vast quantities of American arms and tanks. My wife still has the letter in which I say I didn't know how anyone could resist everything that was packed up into that tiny little country!

About three weeks after the landings, we were on our way across the Channel. We landed at Omaha Beach on June 26th. I was attached to the Psychological War Division. We wore their spade insignia, which we'd dubbed "the shit shovel", on the collars of our uniforms. After driving from the coast through some liberated villages, we reached the Château de Colombières. That's where we were billeted for about six weeks.

The area surrounding the castle at Colombières was constantly shelled and we'd hear the bombs falling all night long. Once I got very close to the front. For 48 hours I was assigned to a team whose job was to go up to the front lines and to send out pamphlets by cannon. The pamphlets were written in German and told the German soldiers to surrender. At night we dug trenches and slept in them. Being on the front was an impressionable experience. The soldiers who'd been there for weeks said: "Don't worry, as long as you hear the bombs, it's all right. It's when you don't hear them that things are *really* bad."

I had a driver and a sound truck. My main job was to prepare a short news program in French on the progress of the war from the BBC or ABSIE broadcasts. Then I'd go onto the public squares of towns and villages that had recently been liberated and broadcast from the truck. I'd also liven up the program by playing American jazz, dance bands and military marches.

There'd sometimes be hundreds of people who'd come out to listen to me. They'd been deprived of their radio receivers, the T.S.F., under the Germans, and a lot of people still didn't have electricity. I'd start playing music to attract them, then read the latest news bulletins, followed by some more music. We'd talk, too. Everywhere people were warm and hospitable. Relations were excellent between the American troops and the inhabitants.

I remember attending four Bastille Day celebrations in different towns on July 14th. People wept for joy upon hearing the *Marseillaise* for the first time in four years. There were American military bands everywhere. I saw little girls wearing dresses made from parachutes. What hospitality! We were spoiled with *Armagnac, Cognac, Madeira,* red wine and cider.

My work on the truck wasn't easy. I covered more than 3000 miles of territory in eight weeks of constant traveling. We bumped about on dusty roads. But the countryside was beautiful, and everywhere people waved at us. I made a lot of friends among the farmers. I'd sometimes give them a chocolate bar or two and come back with half a dozen fresh eggs.

I remember going to St. Lô. It's located in a hollow, with hills on both sides. Before it was liberated, the Germans used to bomb from one side and the Americans from the other. Then one morning we heard "St. Lô is freed," so we went in. There was nothing left, not even the cathedral. Fortunately, most of the inhabitants had left the town. There was absolutely nobody in the streets, and the atmosphere was eerie. We drove through St. Lô in the morning with the sun shining and then again at night with the moonlight on it. It was really a horrifying sight.

In August, another man from the Psychological War Division and I were named to bring out a French news sheet, which we distributed in all the towns we visited. We called it *La Guerre au jour le jour*, which means "The War Day by Day." I might mention we worked very closely with the Civil Affairs Officers of the U.S. Army in many of these towns.

I was often invited for dinner at people's homes. I remember in Granville a French high school English teacher, a widower, invited me and my driver for a fantastic meal. He brought out three bottles of Bordeaux wine, two white and one red, two bottles of champagne cider, a good Calvados and a bottle of Armagnac, which he opened just for me. My driver was a boy from the U.S. south and belonged to a religious group which forbade the consumption of alcoholic beverages. How unhappy the poor English teacher was every time the boy refused to drink!

On one drive along the coast near Mont St. Michel, I remember passing Eisenhower's jeep.

Then on August 18th I received a military order to leave for Paris. My job informing the civilian population was over. Riding in convoy we got as far as Chartres, when the truck broke down because the driver had forgotten to put in oil! I was really impressed: The army was so well-equipped that within two or three hours a new engine was put in and we were off again. While I was waiting, I remember seeing Chartres Cathedral without any stained-glass windows. Apparently, they'd been taken down for safety reasons. It was extraordinary to see the Cathedral with transparent glass. You could see all the statues inside.

On the night of August 24th, I remember sleeping inside a barn in Fontainebleau with some French soldiers. They were of the Leclerc division and were off to liberate Paris the next day. While there, I witnessed an unforgettable scene: A small French boy of about ten presented the French soldiers with a skinned rabbit and a bottle of red wine. The soldiers made a wood fire, cut up the rabbit and cooked it in the wine over a fire, in one of their helmets!

This was in fact just one more use of our helmets. We wore them during the day for protection, of course. During the night we used them as pee-pots, and in the morning, after rinsing them, we filled them with hot water and used them for shaving.

The next day we approached the outskirts of Paris. By that time I was riding in a jeep and carrying a rifle, as there were still snipers everywhere. Paris was liberated during the day, and we were given orders to go in about 9 or 10 o'clock at night. We drove past the Opera and were let out in front of the Hotel Scribe. It was about two in the morning. I immediately called my mother-in-law, who lived in Colombes with her husband. I said, *"Bonjour, c'est Sim.* I'm in Paris." And she answered, *"C'est toi, chéri!"* Her husband was very jealous and wanted to know who this *chéri* was. (...)

Copans' wife Lucienne saved all the letters he sent home during the war. Because of military censorship, place names in the letters were disguised: Copans spoke of Normandy, for example, as "the province that bears the name of a big steamship." The letters abound with affection for France and the local population. Lucienne also still has the sand and a shell he gathered for her upon landing at Omaha Beach.

Remaining in Paris after the War, Sim Copans worked first for Voice of America and then U.S.Information Service. During this time, he collaborated with the French radio and broadcast numerous weekly programs of American symphonic works, Negro spirituals and American folk and popular music. Resigning from the State Department in 1954, Copans went to work for the Radio Diffusion Française . His programs, "Panorama du Jazz Américain", "Jazz en Liberté" and "Deep River", became popular throughout France and also on the Swiss radio network and Radio Monte Carlo. In a radio career that lasted from 1946 to 1975, Copans broadcast more than 4000 programs. In 1975 he created a jazz festival in Souillac, in the southwestern Lot region of France. Renamed "the Sim Copans Festival" in 1985, it continues to attract music lovers every July .

But Sim Copans the radio man and jazz specialist, was also Dr. Simon Copans. A Ph.D. graduate of Brown University (his dissertation was on cultural relations between France and the United States in the 19th century), he lectured for years at various French universities on the history of American music and the origins of jazz. In addition to every corner of France, these lectures also took him to French-speaking countries in Africa. He wrote two books in French, one an anthology of American poetry, J'entends l'Amérique qui chante, *and the other on American protest songs,* Chansons de Revendication, *as well as articles for the scholarly press. In 1960, in collaboration with the American Embassy of Paris, he founded the Institute of American Studies, which would later be attached to the State University of New York. Copans directed, and lectured on American literature and history at, the Institute between 1960 and 1980. He was one of the founding members of the French American Studies Association and helped create this association's scholarly review. He was an administrator, and was on the Board of, the American Library of Paris.*

Copans was a well-known and extremely popular figure in France, both in university circles and among the general public. In recognition for his work in radio and in the field of American Studies, he was awarded two medals by the Legion of Honor.(Chevalier in 1957 and Officer in 1982). In 1985, he became Commander of the Order of Arts and Letters, and in 1988 the University of Nancy awarded him the Docteur Honoris Causa *degree.*

For many years, Sim and Lucienne Copans shared their time between Paris and their home at Lanzac, in the Lot. Sim died on February 22, 2000. He is survived by Lucienne and their two sons – one an anthropologist and Professor of Sociology at the University of Amiens, the other a producer of documentary films – and four grandchildren.

Two french boys

In April 1944, two French brothers, Charles and Aubert Lemeland, respectively twelve and eleven years old, left their home in La Haye-du-Puits with their parents to join the exodus from this strategic town. A devastated La Haye would later be taken from the Germans by the 1st Battalion of the 314th Regiment of the American army on July 8.

Memories of that summer have never left the two Lemeland brothers. In 1990 Charles wrote an article about that time for the alumni bulletin of St. Paul's School. In extracts from that article, he recounts what it was like living in La Haye-du-Puits under the Occupation, his family's journey to safer territory and his boyhood impressions of the American GI's.

As for Aubert, he remembers the war in his music (he is a composer), his poetry and his oral accounts of the time.

<u>Charles Lemeland</u>

The German army arrived in La Haye-du-Puits on June 18, 1940, with the villagers in a state of panic, confusion and disbelief. The archenemy was arriving! People did not know what to expect and therefore expected the worst. Most of the villagers left and took shelter in the neighboring farms.

German soldiers were in our house when we came out of hiding. They left after a few days but kept the top floor for the remainder of the war. An officer and his orderly lived there. They were generally quiet, stiffly polite. Some spoke excellent French.(...)

For adults, the Occupation was a trying time. Their pride had been badly harmed by a sudden and complete defeat. I think they spent the whole war in a state of apprehension and intermittent *ennui*. For young boys, the war was more often than not, I confess, interesting, even thrilling, although the lack of toys and candy was at times an unpleasant consideration. But the war wore on, bringing a curfew, arrests, some deportations. A man was shot running away from German sentries. Some fled to join the Resistance somewhere else in France. By 1943 the German army no longer looked invincible. Late that year, I think, radio sets had to be turned in to the German authorities so that we could not hear the good news on the B.B.C. A very few times an English fighter plane (American planes made their appearance in the skies only in 1944) swooped low over the village and strafed the railroad station. It made a lot of noise and was big talk for the rest of the day.(...)

In La Haye, by the end of April 1944, although life had a semblance of normalcy (the theater was still showing movies), there was much fear and anxiety. On the 26th, 27th and 28th of April, A-20 "Boston" light bombers bombed the railroad station. Some bombs ended up in the wrong places. Our German "boarders" told us that we should leave. Mademoiselle Poulain, who taught us English with a touching eagerness that we did not appreciate, was angry because we did not study. We would not be able to say *deux mots* to the Americans, she said. (...) That was the end of the English classes. On April 29th, taking the cat and the two dogs, we left La Haye for the countryside in Glatigny, five miles away.

It is there that we heard about the Allied landings, on a gray, cool, and tense Tuesday. It was not a surprise. The night before there had been tremendous activity in the air. The several hundred planes taking the paratroopers to their destination had passed in the vicinity, as we discovered much later. The Americans had landed, we were told, but that raised a number of questions. When would they arrive in Glatigny? How did American soldiers really look? What kind of uniform did they wear? What guns and equipment would they have?

What would their faces be like? What was their style as soldiers? We had to wait exactly one month for the answers. (...)

On July 5th at 11:30 a.m. (according to my father's little diary) old Emery Luce came to the field where we and two other families had spent the previous three days. "*Les Américains sont là,*" he said. Everybody knew then that it was time to get out. At the first crossroads there was an armored car with a big white star on it. The man in the turret did not even seem to notice us as we walked by.

At a cluster of houses nearby, a little celebration was going on. All sorts of vehicles were on the road. Soldiers and French people were exchanging greetings. We got some chewing gum but had no idea what it was. That the "new" soldiers gave us something was a very pleasant surprise. We never got anything from German soldiers, or French soldiers, for that matter. At the house of Madame Holley we had steaks and French tries.

There was great rejoicing. It was short-lived, though. The Americans were now in the process of setting up their own mortars and machine guns, and they told us we should leave. From every direction, it seemed, came the dangerous and incoherent murmur of war, building up, slowing down, starting again, breaking out in absurd and wild starts. But where were the Germans? Where were the lines? It was a strange summer tableau. In spite of the noise, or perhaps because of it, the sunny countryside looked even more dead, abandoned, frightening. Familiar places appeared unrecognizable, for it seemed there was now something horrible and monstrous hiding there. The endless road, bordered here and there by houses and farms, was absolutely deserted but for dead animals – a German shepherd and a pig side by side – and a few dead men. Spread over miles was the simple ordinary war garbage: that is, everything – clothing, food, ammunition – an immense yard sale gone crazy.

At the end of our journey was Barneville, one of the rare small towns left totally unscathed by the fighting armies. It was teeming with activity and full of Americans. Friendly, good humored, and good-looking, they were quite popular, especially with women. Best of all, they did not look or act like fanatical, professional soldiers. As if they did not take the war quite seriously or, at least, not all the time. They had a great talent for enjoying themselves whenever they could. We were fascinated by their demeanor, their gestures. In a word, they were "cool". The way they got into their cars and drove was classy, with a touch of wildness. We could not figure out why they threw balls at each other endlessly or why they would want to use those ridiculously big gloves. Strange soldiers. Right in the middle of a campaign, they had time to play. They were definitely a different breed of cats.

The baggy shape of the American uniform was another surprise. We were used to the tight-fitting garments of the Wehrmacht. Black hobnailed boots were now replaced by a soft, civilized walking item often covered by those strange canvas leggings. Armies have their own particular smell. The German soldier combined those of leather, soap and tea. Not bad, but no match for the precious and novel perfumery the American army had to offer: peppermint, doughnut and American tobacco.

What impressed us most was the U.S. war material. First, the unimaginable quantities: thousands of trucks and cars. German military vehicles always had a wickedly purposeful look. Compared to the mean-looking Panther tank, the American Sherman did seem rather laid back, like an unaggressive crustacean. American trucks and cars were like civilian trucks and cars that had been painted to assume a warlike stance. That cocky, lovable little jeep was an immediate hit. Made for war but maybe for fun also! We were dying to get a ride in one. My sister, who was in a boarding school and had not been heard of since the end of May, was brought back to us by an officer of the U.S. Army Civilian Branch. She made a splendid appearance in a jeep. She was the lucky one!

One morning, late in July, when we had settled down at a relative's house, we woke up to find the woods around us, the Forest of St. Sauveur-Le-Vicomte, alive with bivouacking soldiers of the U.S. 3rd Army. A good number of these soldiers were New Englanders, and some spoke a French dialect that we had little difficulty understanding. We children had always remained at a safe distance from the German soldiers. Not that we were afraid of them, but rather because they represented another form of adult authority which did not appear to really understand us or at least had limited patience with us. We did not trust them, just as we did not trust any teacher and many adults. With the American soldiers it was the wonderful world of laughter, play, and permissiveness: candy galore, the thrill of getting inside tanks and other fascinating machinery and touching all those levers and pedals, posing for pictures, looking at pictures of relatives, of girlfriends usually in bathing suits and appearing to us like movie stars! We wondered if it was sinful to even look at them. Would we have to mention that in confession?

The soldiers stayed about a week, I think. And it was one of the most exciting weeks of my life. My brother and I visited *les Américains* from morning to night. We came home with unimaginable gifts: a pair of army boots that hopefully, in a year or two, would fit me, loads of things to eat, all as well-packaged as perfume bottles, and, greatest of all, a small tent. The Eldorado had come to us. The Americans were nothing but demi-gods haloed with a kind of supernatural prestige.

One evening, two demi-gods came for dinner, Roland Chareat of Nashun, New Hampshire, and Victor Bouvier of Marlboro, Massachusetts. I don't know how my uncle had succeeded in inviting them. He was a very warm and convincing man. My father was surprised that soldiers about to go to battle would accept such an invitation. My aunt was a great cook and made a very fine meal. The women in the house thought that the two Americans were charming and most handsome. I was in awe.

After the war we went back many, many times to the woods of St. Sauveur, to hunt rabbits and birds. The woods now seemed strangely empty and dead, white they had been so full of life, activity and excitement during that wonderful week in July 1944. Now it is a rendezvous for memories and nostalgia. Some years ago you could still trace little ondulations, little waves on the ground where foxholes had been dug. Maybe they are still there today. Little ripples left by a little moment of history.

Aubert Lemeland

I was only eleven at the time, but many images of the German occupation of La Haye-du-Puits have remained in my memory. When the Germans were living in our house, I remember that one day an officer asked my mother if he could "play some notes". We had, it must be said, a Gaveau piano in the living-room. My mother let him play. My brother and I hid in the hall to listen and watch him through the glass French doors. At Christmas, the officers, who never stayed long at our house, would receive packages. Once in awhile, the orderly would offer us a piece of cake that was "made in Germany". This was at the beginning of the occupation. As the months passed, and with each military setback, the atmosphere changed.

My father's diary mentions that on July 5th we met the first American soldiers to arrive in Glatigny, a village located several kilometers from La-Haye-du-Puits. As if it were yesterday, I remember a small armored car with large tires and a little cannon assembled with other vehicles at an intersection. Almost immediately, Americans and Norman farmers were fraternizing. Hidden old bottles were brought out and passed around – an improvised banquet where everyone is standing, glass in hand. These are powerful images that haven't dimmed with time. Everyone was radiant with joy to have rediscovered freedom. Nothing complicated. It was just enough to be with U.S. soldiers along a Norman road.

The road we were on was what we then called a "Coutances road". It was large, lined with tall, straight trees, and had grass in the middle. The landscape was somewhat Corot-like. These soldiers came from the 313th regiment of the 79th Division. They were very friendly. We gave them cider, even if at that time of the year it was a rather stiff drink!

All these men in uniform came from so far away. In the photos taken on the beach, which we saw later on, they give the impression of emerging from the ocean! With their gear, their tanks and their large, open-mouthed boats in the distance, they resembled modern knights. Eisenhower called his memoirs "The European Crusade", which I find a very good title.

We left Glatigny for Barneville, where we stayed about ten days. We would go to the public square of this small town to listen to the news being broadcast from a military truck. I learned recently that the Information Officer of the 1st Army who was in the truck was Sim Copans. The news was not always good for refugees. The outcome of the Battle of Caen, which was in the British sector, was still uncertain. Sim Copans also broadcast music. In America, at the time, it was the golden age of the big dance bands. We would especially listen to Glen Miller and the Modernaires, but I'm sure we also heard the Dorsey brothers, Charlie Barnet, "In the Mood" and "Tampico".

Later, in Cherbourg, in September, I remember concerts given in the bandstand of the *Place Napoléon* by the army bands. I was in seventh-heaven, turning around the bandstand, hearing all the different sounds of an orchestra. We didn't recognize any of the pieces being played – John Philip Sousa's medleys or the arrangements of Gershwin's tunes.

In Cherbourg we lived near the *Place Napoléon,* which looked out on the beach – still barred to the public – and the seaport. In the distance could be seen a multitude of Liberty Ships and mountains of military supplies. The equestrian statue of Napoléon pointing his finger towards England had disappeared under crates of equipment. Liberated on June 27th without much destruction, Cherbourg several months later swarmed with soldiers, airmen and sailors. The largest store in the city had been transformed into a PX, a noisy drugstore off limits to civilians. We'd try our luck at begging for doughnuts, which we were very fond of. Black soldiers would give us some.

I also remember that the itinerant fairs came back in force in Cherbourg then. Driving a little car for a few minutes was intoxicating – a rare moment of happiness. The GIs often asked us to accompany them in these minuscule vehicles. Playing in the background above the din was an incredible mixture of French songs and North American rhythms. The Americans were unbelievably "successful" among French girls. There's no other way to say this. My sister, who was only fifteen, didn't stop talking about them with her friends from school. My brother and I would see them endlessly plotting how to get close to the young liberators.

Retrospectively, this was probably the strongest, the most intense period of my life. There was no room for lukewarm feelings. All at once we learned what fear, and even terror, was. We were mere witnesses, however, not the actors, of the drama. The actors were all those soldiers whose eyes we met – and who were heading towards hell, death, their own death.

Soon afterwards, I returned to the classroom and then went on to secondary school. But all these events were still too close in time. I round the Greek myths and Corneille's tragedies mere incidentals. This feeling has never left me. I couldn't stand having the page turned so quickly. Out of affinity and sympathy for all those soldiers. We owe our birth to our parents, but we also owe our survival – there are always exceptional circumstances in life – to people who permitted you to continue to breathe because they were placed there, at a certain moment of their lives, to defend you, and even die to save you. There's nothing stronger than that. When I see the pictures of the beaches with these men rising from the ocean, this image becomes an obsession for me. June 6, 1944 – Anne Frank notes it in her diary – is also a date of hope, hope for all those who are in the camps. All these waves of assault on the Normandy beaches are like the declension of the word freedom, its first syllable.

Ever since that time, I have remained mistrustful of words, of written work, of speech. Between 1940 and 1944 in France and in occupied Europe, you could harm someone with ill-chosen words and threaten his or her existence by an ambiguous text. From an internment camp, they would be transferred to a death camp. Openly implying or writing that a certain person was Jewish meant their death warrant. You never saw them again. During the war, words were fearsome and their meaning to be feared. Let us not forget the collaborators' deceitful abominations on the radio in Vichy.

Music allowed me to express everything without a text, with no words. Nowadays, though, I'm reverting to vocal music. I find it a great homecoming, and it makes me very happy to rediscover the human voice. It brings me back to what I knew during the war. I now also write my own texts about this period. My debt of gratitude is still intense. I remember.

THE LEMELAND BROTHERS

Fascinated by America ever since the war, Charles Lemeland emigrated to the United States in 1954. After working briefly on Wall Street, he attended Columbia University, where he obtained a Master's degree in history, and the Sorbonne, from which he received a doctorate. Beginning his teaching career in 1961, he has taught at various schools and universities in the United States. He has been on the faculty of St. Paul's School in Concord, New Hampshire, since 1974. He and his wife have two daughters. The owners of a 19th-century mill on the Cotentin peninsula in Normandy, they return frequently to France for their summer holidays.

Aubert Lemeland, a well-established composer in France, has written seven symphonies and a number of other works, including "Elegy to the Memory of Samuel Barber" and "An American Epitaph to the Memory of Aaron Copland." A great admirer of American music, he says he heard American composers, jazz and big band music for the first time from Sim Copans' sound truck in Barneville and listening to U.S. army bands in Cherbourg during the War. One of his

latest works puts to music his poem "Omaha"[1] and the war poems of
six American poets. Lemeland lives in Paris.

The Forest of Saint-Sauveur

    In green meadows
    And hamlets forked by hedge
    Where the mists of November
    Are scattered about the glades
    Chapped and bitten by the autumn frost,

    Burdening trees encased, their limbs bare,
    Copses wettened
    And bathed in dew.
    In the morning sunlight
    Oak, full elm and tall beech,
    Refuge of the winged flight
    Of silent September.

    Still forest of Saint Sauveur,
    I remember...
    Those white stars between the leaves
    An entire army under the grove
    Drowsily sleeping and waking:
    Artus and Robin Hood
    In the heather of Claude Debussy.

    Toward other meadows, other forests
    The Sleeping Army would go
    The Sleeping Army setting forth
    Afar, toward the heavy sobs
    Of the guns of summer.

AUBERT LEMELAND
(Translated by Hilary Kaiser)

---

(1) A translation of this poem is found under "Those Left Behind".

Major Ridgway B. Knight recevant la *Légion d'honneur* en Italie, 1944

Major Ridgway B. Knight receiving the *Légion d'honneur* in Italy, 1944

Major Ridgway B. Knight, circa 2000.

William Jay Smith avec son père
à Schofield Barracks, Hawaï, 1942

William Jay Smith with his father at
Schofield Barracks, Hawaii, 1942

S.S. La Grandière

R. Lantagne, *commander* du Post N° 1
de l'*American Legion*

R. Lantagne, commander American
Legion Post N° 1

De gauche à droite (from left to right) : général de
Lattre de Tassigny, général Juin, *major* Ridgway
B. Knight, général Clark et le général de Gaulle

Ted Liska, Normandie, 1944

Ted Liska, Normandy 1944

Sergent Ted Liska with President Dwight Eisenhower, 1963

Sergeant Ted Liska aux côtés du président Dwight Eisenhower, 1963

Hilary Kaiser avec (de gauche à droite) messieurs Kurtz, Lantagne, Lemeland, au moment de la sortie de la première édition de *Veteran Recall*, à la librairie Brentano's, à Paris

Colin Powell et Ted Liska à *Omaha Beach*

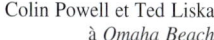

Des aviateurs à la ferme des Adam. Gus Bubenzer (debout à gauche), Gene Young (debout au milieu), Henry Hodulick (à genoux, au milieu).

Airmen at the Adamses' Farm: Gus Bubenzer (standing left), Gene Young (standing middle) and Henry Hodulick (kneeling middle)

Maurice Quillien (portant la bannière) et des camarades de Résistance du 1er bataillon de l'Armée française, en 1944.

Maurice Quillien (holding banner) and fellow resistants in the First Battalion of the French Army, 1944.

Sim Copans
U.S. First Army camp,
England, June 1944

Sim Copans et son camion sonorisé (à bord d'un navire de débarquement, juin 1944).

Sim Copans and his sound truck (aboard an LST, June 1944)

Charles & Aubert Lemeland,
La Haye-du-Puits, 1942

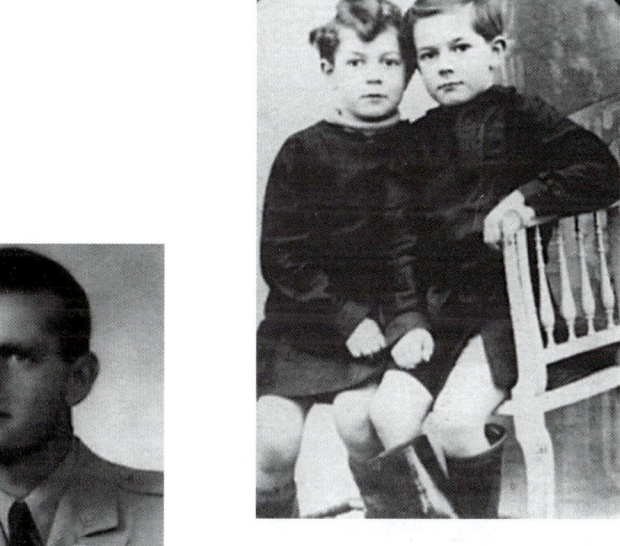

George Hook

John Davis, (*commander* du Post
N° 605 du VFW).

John Davis, today

John Davis, 1944
(now Commander of VFW Post No 605)

Eugene Kurtz

Warren Trabant (pendant une immobilisation de la colonne).

Warren Trabant (during a delay in the column)

François Mitterrand, ministre des Anciens Combattants, en train de décorer Julius Winter, de la Légion d'honneur, 1948.

François Mitterrand, Minister of War Veterans, decorating Julius Winter, with the *Légion d'honneur*, 1948

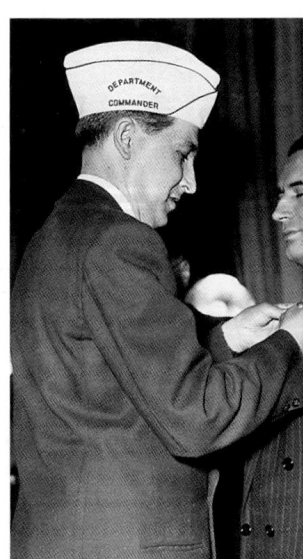

Julius Winter et (and) le général Leclerc

Phyllis Michaux
Camp Upton, New York, 1944

Phyllis Michaux et des amies, Paris, 1945

Phyllis Michaux and friends, Paris, 1945

Phyllis Michaux et ses amies

Phyllis Michaux and her friends

Champs-Élysées

Défilé militaire du Service
féminin de l'Armée
américaine sur les
Champs-Élysées,
6 juin 1945.

Military parade of
Women's Army Corps,
Champs-Élysées,
June 6, 1945

The tank commander

Born in Middleton, Ohio, in 1919, George Hook was planning to come and work for Morgan Bank in Paris just after graduation from Yale University. When the War broke out in 1939, however, his passport was canceled, so he went to work in Kansas City for ARMCO, the steel corporation his grandfather had founded in 1900. Then, in 1943, he enlisted in the Army.

I tried to enlist in the Navy and Air Corps, but they said I couldn't see, so I volunteered for the Army, who said I had 2020 vision! After "boot camp" I volunteered for the armored forces – better to ride than walk – and was sent to Fort Knox Officers' School, Louisville, Kentucky, where I graduated a "90-day wonder" as a 2nd Lieutenant.

One day when I was out in the field on a training exercise, the sergeant carne out in his jeep and informed me I was off for the desert. I thought the desert was Africa. So did the sergeant. It turned out to be California! So I went out to the California desert as Asst. G.3, Planning, on the staff of General Murphy, Commanding General of the 7th Armored Division.

After maneuvers one day, when we were back east getting ready to go to France, I went to see the General. I told him that, as I really didn't know much about being an officer, I'd really like to go down to one of the line battalions. This was my downfall. When I turned up at the headquarters of the regiment my battalion was attached to, the Colonel said, "What the hell did you do, Lieutenant! The General gave you such a disastrous performance report, your career in this man's army is finished as far as promotion is concerned." It seems General Murphy took my request to leave his staff as a personal insult and so "blacklisted" me in the report he sent down to Colonel McConnell. Quite frankly, I didn't care.

Before coming to France, our staging area in England was on the Salisbury plains southwest of London. It was there that the 7th Armored Division joined the 3rd Army under General Patton. I remember seeing the General for the first time in London. He was wearing his pearl-handled pistols and all. He and General Walker, the second in command, had got all of us out on a football field and were making speeches to build up the troops. I remember thinking at the time, if a bomb falls on this football field, the whole U.S. Army has had it.

I crossed the Channel on an LST, a Landing Ship Tank. As I was the senior officer – Colonel McConnell had managed to make me a 1st Lieutenant by then – the British naval officer running the ship declared, with tongue in cheek, that I was in charge. I remember telling him if that was the case, I suggested we turn the ship around and head back home! We continued on our way, landing on Utah Beach.

After landing, we made our way through Sainte-Mère-Eglise and on to Coutance and Avranches, where we turned east in the direction of Paris. The 3rd Army was divided into two tank forces. I was a platoon leader of Company A. My platoon became "the point", followed by the battalion, the regiment and the army. This meant I was riding in the front tank most of the time until I got shot up just outside Metz.

The Colonel would drive up to my tank in his jeep. He'd just tell me what road to take and to keep on going until he ordered me to stop. So all of our tanks would go tearing down the road, and the Germans would run after us, and we'd run after them. We kept on going, like steam rollers preparing a path for those coming behind.

I used to travel with the turret open or "unbuttoned", as we'd say. If you buttoned it up and used the periscope, you only started seeing anything at 20 feet in front of you. You had a blind spot for anything closer. And with the periscope you just saw ground coming toward you; you couldn't tell what direction you were going.

One of the encounters where the fighting was fierce was at the town of Senonches, southwest of Dreux. On the other side of the town was a German ammunition dump which our planes had been bombing. For protection, the German troops were in trenches. When we appeared they ran for their 88 artillery guns. Fortunately, my gunner got them before they got us, and we fought our way into town. In the melee we lost four tanks.

Most of the men in the tanks were able to get out in time. I tried to save the driver of the fourth tank, but he was already dead by the time I got to him. It's horrible what could happen to you in a tank. A heavy shell would get into the tank and smash you like a hydraulic hammer. And then the shell would set off your own ammunition.

By that time it was dark and no one knew who was doing what to whom. Communications were more than confused. Not having been told anything different, my boys and I fought our way through the town, destroying several German tanks, until we carne to a clearing near a woods. I decided it was best to stay there until morning. So we circled our tanks round, covered-wagon style, to wait until dawn. About that time, I received a call over the intercom from the Colonel saying, "Hook, stop the advance. We'll take the town in the morning." "Too late," I replied. "The town has already been took!"

I must say it was an emotional thrill to liberate a French town. After the fighting was over and all the Germans had been killed or captured, or had fled, the streets were suddenly filled with joyous crowds of people who appeared from nowhere. We were offered everything and anything they had in the way of food and drink. A lot of Calvados, I seem to remember. In one town a pretty young girl climbed up on my tank and presented me with a small French flag she had made and kept for the day of liberation. It is still one of my most treasured possessions.

While it was tremendous being in the center of such crowds of happy people, it was also terrifying because you never knew when the German tanks might reappear. Our guns were always loaded and ready to shoot. My fear was that a gunner of one of my tanks might accidentally pull the trigger, and that would have meant disaster, with many people killed.

We forged on through Dreux and on to Paris. We didn't go into Paris, as we were told to hold up and let General Leclerc have the honor. So we went south of Paris and made a formal crossing of the Seine via a pontoon bridge at Ponthierry, just north of Melun. I believe our division was the first army unit to cross the Seine.

After crossing the Seine River we headed for Château Thierry. I was again "the point". We fought our way into and through the town, taking and holding the strategic bridge over the Marne River. We held the town over night while being bombarded by German artillery and air force. Our losses were quite heavy.

The following day, while our task force was en route from Château Thierry, the Colonel called to tell me to head to Rheims. We had no maps or intelligence at that point and were going so fast I hadn't the slightest idea where Rheims was. Fortunately, a little boy on a bicycle came out of the woods, whereupon I got out of the tank and in my best French asked him the direction to Rheims. "Follow me," he said. So off we went – me at the point, followed by the Task Force and the whole 3rd Army! Wish I'd had a camera. All I could think of was the passage in the Bible, "and a little Child shall lead them."

The Colonel called again and said to head for Epernay and Châlons-sur-Marne. In Châlons, we ran into two companies of German foot soldiers. They had no idea the Americans were any-where around. They simply surrendered, and we turned them over to our troops. Then on to Sainte-Ménéhould, where we ran into a new problem. Not only were there Germans on the ground, but also Germans on roofs of the buildings shooting down at us and throw-ing teller land mines off the buildings. It was sort of like the Far West. However, "the good guys" got the best of "the bad guys", and the Colonel was on the intercom shouting, "Keep going."

Outside Clermont-en-Argonne, the Colonel called down to tell me to find a bivouac area where the Combat Command could hole up for the night since it was already dark. No sooner had I located a seemingly suitable spot than the Colonel called again. "Keep going," he said. "We're going to take Verdun!" All I could think of was the First World War and the millions of troops that had been killed. And here we were going to take the city at night with no intelligence and the force of a Combat Command!

So, off we went full speed ahead until we rounded a corner and found ourselves at a railroad crossing. Then there was the flash of an 88. We tried to shoot back but had no idea where the German tank was. The second shot hit the tank, and it blew up. Two of the boys were killed. I found myself on the road. Dragging myself to a ditch, I could see big flames coming out of the turret. Lying next to the tank was one of my crew members. He was calling, "Lieutenant! Lieutenant!" There were German voices shouting in the background. I crawled over to my crewman and told him to put his hands around my neck and hold on. I crawled back over to the ditch on my hands and knees with the crewman holding onto my neck. By that time, all hell was breaking loose. There was gunfire everywhere, from tanks to 155 howitzers. Not having any intelligence, the Colonel decided to call off the attack until morning.

If we'd had intelligence and kept on going, the war just might have ended a little sooner, since the German General Staff under Kesselring was in Verdun. But, by the time the fighting was over in the morning and we had taken the town, the General Staff had gone east!

That was the end of the advance from Avranches to Verdun. We were out of gas! I had tanks everywhere. Not only was Combat Command A stopped, but so was the whole Third Army. We remained in Verdun for seven long days, allowing the Germans time to retreat and consolidate their positions.

I remember when I first went into the city. Some French people came running out of their houses and offered us a bottle. I took a sip, but it was so strong, I felt my whole throat burning. I felt I had to drink it, though. I guess it was *Schnapps*.

Finally, we were off again, headed for Metz, an old fortress town that was held and strengthened by the Germans. En route, my tank was blown up by a land mine, and I had to hop on another one. We didn't have any idea where we were and ended up as sitting ducks on the firing range of Metz's heavy duty guns. Once again, all hell broke loose. All we could see were the gun flashes coming from the Fort. We tried, but couldn't shoot back. Then the Germans started shooting shrapnel shells that exploded above ground. That was the end for me. I'd put my head over the turret, and the next thing I knew I was lying at the bottom of the tank with a broken neck. Fortunately, when I heard the gunner call over the radio, "Lieutenant Hook is dead. We're getting the hell out of here," I was able to open my eyes and wink weakly at the boys to let them know I wasn't quite as dead as they thought. Then I passed out. They got the tank away from the shelling, and I was carried off to a field hospital.

This was September. I stayed for awhile in French and English hospitals and then landed up for four months in an army hospital in Louisville, Kentucky. My career as a tank officer ended where it had all begun, not very many months earlier.

In June 1945 War Correspondent Ira Wolfert wrote an article about Hook's exploits, entitled "The War from Inside a Tank," for The Reader's Digest. *Hook was awarded the Silver Star, the Bronze Star, the Purple Heart, the croix de Guerre and the medal of Verdun.*

After the war ended, Hook came to work for ARMCO in Paris. He was going to stay for a year, but, as he then said, "that was 44 years ago!" He retired as European Vice-President of the company in 1984.

Hook was an active member, and a former warden, of the American Cathedral of Paris. He and his wife, Rosalie, would spend six-months of the year in France on their renovated 17th-century farm in Normandy.

George Hook died on March 18, 2000.

The ordnance officer

When the U.S. entered the war after Pearl Harbor was declared, John Davis, who was born in 1919 in Oakland, California, was a senior at the University of California, Berkeley, studying for a B.S. degree in business. Joining the army, he was sent to officers' candidate school and was commissioned in 1943. He and three other officers then formed a new maintenance company in Pomona, California. Its specific job was to maintain all kinds of equipment, from small arms and artillery to wheel and track vehicles. From there they went to Fort Leonard Wood in Missouri for advanced training and to Tennessee for maneuvers. In early 1944, they were sent to New York and shipped to England on the Queen Mary.

We landed in a port outside Glasgow and were almost immediately sent by train to a town near Norwich in East Anglia. We were being prepared for something, but we didn't know when or where it would be. After hearing the landings had been made in Normandy, we were told to get ready. While we were being moved from East Anglia to Portsmouth, we were told that we had to stay in Oxfordshire until further notice. So we stayed in Oxfordshire for at least three weeks and didn't sail to France until late July.

Before arriving in Oxfordshire, we'd been told to waterproof all our vehicles. We had to hand cover every part that could be reached by water with a plastic coating. We'd done this very conscientiously, and every single one of the vehicles was ready to go. But when we arrived near Oxford, we were told there was a shortage of waterproofing material, so we had to take off all the waterproofing from our vehicles and ship it to the ports. Later on, we were told to re-waterproof our vehicles and, believe it or not, once again they told us to unwaterproof them!

It was pretty frustrating. The ironic thing, too, is that after we got to Portsmouth and embarked on an LST, I started talking to one of the Navy men on board. The Navy had been running a sort of "ferry boat" service back and forth to Normandy for about six weeks, and I thought he would know what the situation was. I said, "You know, we've made a tremendous effort to have our vehicles waterproofed. How much water do you think we're actually going to have?" And he replied, sardonically, "Well, when we've landed, if you walk out about 150 yards *behind* the ship you might find a little dampness." And he was right. We arrived at Utah Beach at high tide, but by the time we got the orders to land, the tide had gone out and we could just roll across the sand high and dry! All that waterproofing proved to be completely useless!

We disembarked at Utah Beach on July 28th, just before the break-through had been made at Avranches. From there we moved up to a little town near Valognes and then on to Cherbourg. Leaving Cherbourg on August 15th, we were sent to Bricquebec and La Haye-du-Puits on the Cotentin west coast. Our company the 3528th, with about 224 men, wasn't attached to any particular battalion. We'd be given orders to report to a certain battalion for a week and then to another the following week. We wanted to get ourselves attached to a corps and to leave Normandy, but that never happened. Camping out in foxholes, we stayed on the Cotentin peninsula until mid-October.

I remember an incident that occurred while we were in one of the towns on the Cotentin peninsula. Food was really short then for the local population, so after we went through the chow line, the cooks would often ladle out what was left over to some little French kids who came around with their buckets. One kid used to be there, late at night and in the morning, all the time. So some of us tried to ask him, in our broken French, why he didn't go home. He told us he didn't have a home, his parents had been killed, his older sister had a German boyfriend and all these people were menacing her, so he'd decided to take off.

In our company there was a man who'd been a tailor in civilian life, so he fixed up a little uniform for the guy, who thought he was king of the heap. He'd play the first sergeant when the French kids got into the chow line and give them orders. We used to get a big kick out of it. One of the men went to the company commander and told him he and his wife had no children and they wanted to adopt the little guy. The company commander agreed, and so we went down to the local *Mairie* to fill in the papers. They wanted all the information we had and told us to come back with the boy. So we brought him to the town hall in his uniform, and the mayor sat us all down in a big room. Then the door opened and out came the boy's mother and father! It turned out the boy had run away from home and made up the whole story to be with the soldiers and to play at being a big shot. There was no older sister, no German boyfriend, it was all complete fabrication. When he saw his parents, he broke into tears, saying he didn't mean to do any harm and whatnot. All of us thought it was a good joke – everybody, of course, but one guy.

Sometime in October, the company commander gave me the mission of finding a suitable place for the company to spend the winter. After making a survey of Granville, I decided it would do and requisitioned a hotel, where the men were quartered until the rest of the war. We officers – a captain and three of us lieutenants – took over a vacation cabin called "O Sole Mio".

We were later told to leave the "O Sole Mio" and move into the most amazing place. It was a huge fancy home that looked just like a château. It had been a Gestapo headquarters for several years and was subsequently taken over by General Bradley, who had it fitted out with all the necessary communications equipment. By the way, General Eisenhower's headquarters were also in the area, in Jullouville, several kilometers south of Granville. But the war went so quickly – and Paris was captured so quickly – that they didn't have to have a rear echelon on the coast, so they moved General Bradley to Versailles. He wasn't so sure he wouldn't be back, though, if the army had to retreat. So he said he wanted the château occupied with all the communications equipment intact. The U.S. colonel told the mayor of the French town, who wanted to put up refugees in the château, that the army had to hold on to it for tactical reasons. Then he sent the four of us over there to occupy it. It was a big, beautiful estate with a full staff of servants. We found ourselves in luxury we had not only never lived in, but never even believed in. It was pretty shameful, really, with the war going on and all.

What made a very big impression on me – for after all, I was only 24 years old – was my experience working with military justice.

There was a rule that every regiment should have its own tribunal in treating AWOLs and so forth. But there was one exception. If you had civilian witnesses, the wrongdoer had to be tried by the army locally. In very serious cases, there'd be an Article 32 hearing, which is like a grand jury hearing. The men were put into the local jails and later tried by the military after the civilian witnesses had been found and brought into court to testify.

But there weren't enough qualified officers to try these men. So one day in November or December, I was called into headquarters and asked to take over some of these cases. I'd studied commercial law in college and done a little bit of legal work in the army on minor cases, but never any criminal law. And these cases were unbelievable! There were murders, rapes, murder-rape combinations. The investigations had already been made by the army criminal investigation department. I was on the prosecution, my job being to find the civilian witnesses. I'd go into the towns and villages looking for them with an interpreter. A lot of the accused were later executed.

In February of '45 I volunteered for retraining as an infantry officer and was sent to a ground forces retraining course in Fontainebleau for eight weeks. Our instructors were brought over from Fort Benning, from the finest school the army had. The Fort Benning school was called "T.I.S." then – The Infantry School – and it was a model for all other army schools. We were in the first course. The second course was so close to the end of the war that all of these infantry officers were taken as a group and sent down to the Riviera, where they became hotel managers! There were some crazy things that happened in the war.

That reminds me of another crazy incident. There were some soldiers in our company who had very high IQs and they were sent off on a specialized army training program and to colleges to be trained as engineers, doctors, scientists, and so forth. The program was set up as though the war was going to last for ten years. Then in late November '44, the army realized they didn't have enough GIs. So the men who were having Thanksgiving dinner at home in the United States were yanked away, sent over to Europe and taken in as replacements just before the "bulge" was blasted through. These men hadn't even been properly trained. There were incredible losses.

From Fontainebleau we were sent out to Brittany to take over two pockets of German resistance on the coast, at Lorient and St. Nazaire. We were sitting outside Lorient when the war carne to an end, so not a shot was fired. Then from Brittany we were shipped to Germany.

We traveled to Germany in what you call 40 and 8 cars. The origins of the term 40 and 8 go back to World War I. During that time, the French railroad ran out of passenger cars, so they transported troops in box cars on the side of which read: "This car can be used for 40 men or 8 horses." We were loaded into these cars, which, as a matter of fact, were very comfortable. The railroad would put in a bale of straw in each car, and we'd break up the bale and spread the straw around so that we could lay out our bed rolls. It was quite comfortable lying on the floor of the car. Usually in the early morning the train would stop for awhile and we'd run up with our helmets and draw off a little hot water from the locomotive for shaving and washing and so on.

In Germany we were given the option of staying on there and running POW camps or volunteering for service in the Pacific. I opted for the second choice and was shipped out of Antwerp. But en route for New York, we learned that the war was over in the east.

After being discharged at Camp Beale, California, Davis returned to Berkeley. In 1947 and 1948 he went to the Far East on a civilian contract with the Korean military government. Upon his return to the U.S., he entered the shipping and transport business. Having taken a reserve commission in 1945, he found himself recalled into active duty as an infantry officer in 1950 and stationed in Verdun, France as of 1951. He returned to his job with the shipping company in the U.S. in early 1953. After working in Germany for a year, he came to France to live in 1957 and, except for a year in Holland and three years in Iran, has lived in Paris ever since. Retired since 1990, Davis has been Commander of Benjamin Franklin Post No. 605 of the Veterans of Foreign Wars since 1991.

Davis and his French wife, Jeannette, married in Paris in 1951. They have a daughter, a son and two grandchildren.

The soldier from Utah

Carolyn Dupuis' uncle, George W. Coon, was born in Pleasant Green, Utah. After attending high school and studying bookkeeping and accounting, he served as a Mormon missionary in Texas and Louisiana. Coon married Bertha Openshaw in August 1942 and was drafted into the army in March 1943. This piece describes the mood in Carolyn Dupuis' house, her street and her city while Coon was fighting in the infantry in France.

My Uncle George

Aunt Bertha lived in our house
When Uncle George went away to the second world war
And his letters used to arrive three times a week
Until one week there was no letter
Then one month
Then three months

"Heard from George?" was on everybody's lips
"Heard from George?" cried up and down the streets
Arrived shouting through the telephone
Pounding on the door
Scratched at the windows, seeped through the cracks in
    the coal bin wall
And stormed down the chimney
Until finally no one asked

Then somebody spotted Uncle George, they thought, at
     the Salt Lake Rialto

In the News of the World

The projectionist showed us this news twice each night
     for five nights in a row

Once regular speed and once slow motion

And he said he would have shown it upside down and
     backwards too

If that would do any good

Where was it made?

Someplace in the war

When?

Sometime recent

What does recent mean?

In school

We packed boxes

To send to (our teacher said)

All the little children of Europe

Mine had a bar of smelly brown soap

A white wash cloth decorated with blue crosses

A hanky, a comb,

A toothbrush and toothpaste

Would any child anywhere want a toothbrush and toothpaste?

I put a little note in the folds of the hanky,

"If you see my Uncle please send him home".

On our street

Big war stars

Appeared on two of the houses.

Then a letter came from APO New York with the date
   blacked out

But nothing could black out our secret family code

And Uncle George asked if I still had long curls

If he had asked about Mama's garden, it would have
   meant the Philippines

And if he had asked about Daddy's violin, it would have
   meant England

but he asked about me so that meant France.

A long time later the telephone rang

It was Uncle George

His voice as thin as a telephone chord

Calling Aunt Bertha long distance from he wasn't
   allowed to say where

To tell her that almost all of him would soon be home

Can you still love me

Though one of my arms is missing?

Then in a week he knocked on our door with his left hand

And Aunt Bertha fell into his arm saying

Only an arm, George?

And he said

ONLY!

The war ended

We children started playing "Where's Uncle George's Arm?"

Looking under the beds, inside the oven.

Climbing up to the attic, squeezing into the clothes chute,

Crawling into the coal bin and the root cellar

I grew

Left Salt Lake City

Married

Moved to France

Went to Normandy

Visited Utah Beach

Plowed through the sands, shouted at the sea,

Pounded and kicked the bunkers, uprooted flags of grass,

Whispered to all the little white crosses

"Where is Uncle George's Arm?"

And wondered if a bridge I stood under was where
    my newly one-armed

Uncle had hid with his friend

The only 2 survivors of a company of 200

Eventually everybody in our family except Aunt Bertha and
    Uncle George

Went to Utah Beach

They were all looking for something

But Uncle George knew they would never find it.

Carolyn Dupuis

This piece was written following a visit to Utah Beach in 1984. Based on family legend, it describes, or so Dupuis thought, exactly what happened to her uncle during the war, when she was only a little girl. During a phone call to Coon in Salt Lake City, in 1994, however, she discovered that the family had invented some memories! She had been sure that Coon had fought in Normandy. As it turns out, he was in England at the time of the invasion of the

Normandy beaches. He landed in France one month afterwards and was immediately driven to the front line, close to the Moselle River. He was wounded in the Huertgaten forest.

Returning to Utah in March 1945, Coon worked for many years for the Veterans Administration as a claims examiner. He was always an active worker in the Mormon Church and served as a bishop in a Mormon ward for five years. Now retired, he and his wife live in Salt Lake City and have a son, three daughters and many grandchildren .

Carolyn Dupuis was married to a Frenchman and came to France to live in 1969. She died in January 1996 and is survived by André and Isabelle, their dual-national daughter.

BELGIUM, THE NETHERLANDS, GERMANY

The gunner and messenger

Eugene Kurtz was born in Atlanta, Georgia, in 1923. His father, an artist and historian, was an authority on the Atlanta campaign during the Civil War and worked with David O.Selznick as histori-cal advisor for "Gone with the Wind". His grandfather, Captain Fuller, was one of the protagonists in "the Andrews Raid", a his-torical event that took place in 1862 and was later depicted in Buster Keaton's "The General" and in Walt Disney's "The Great Locomotive Chase".

Kurtz knew he wanted to be a composer at the age of nine or ten. He took piano lessons at the age of twelve, but did not begin to study seriously until 1941 at the University of Rochester and the Eastman School of Music. He interrupted his studies to enlist in the army in December 1942.

After eleven weeks of basic training in Macon, Georgia, they gave us all sorts of tests. One was a language aptitude test. And I must have finished it in about twenty minutes because I've always enjoyed languages and have been fairly good at them. So they sent me, along with some of the others, to a program called ASTAP at Fordham University to study German with Jesuit priests. And the priests were absolutely fantastic! They were some of the best teach-ers I've ever come across. We had German from morning to evening, all the time – the language, the history of the country, everything possible. And then, unfortunately, some General, didn't see why we "goof-offs" should be studying languages while other soldiers were dying all over the world. So finally after six months, I think, the orders came through to wipe out the program. And that was an absolute disaster when we eventually arrived in Germany, because we hardly had any people who could speak German!

We were sent to the 104th Infantry Division in Camp Carson, Colorado, and were eventually supposed to be occupation troops. Our general was Terry Allen, who'd had the lst Division but was trounced by Rommel in Africa.

We landed in Cherbourg in August 1944. The port of Cherbourg was full of debris and sunken ships and various things. So we couldn't get into the port of Cherbourg from the ship. We had to be put on barges. Our ship was way out. I think we were the first troops to come directly from the States without going through England.

We first camped at Barneville-sur-Mer in Normandy. Terry Allen wanted to get us into combat because he wanted to get his name back again. Bradley and Patton didn't want him, but he managed to persuade the British and the Canadians, who were further north on the Belgian-Dutch border, to take us. And so, in October, we went into combat with the British and Canadians on the Belgian-Dutch border, at the time of the Arnhem disaster.

I remember our first night in combat, our baptism of fire. I think the various captains who were leading us had never been in combat before, and they must have been trying to do things by the book. And, of course, if you're used to combat, you don't do things by the book. You do things just by analyzing the situation at hand. And so we dutifully dug our fox holes, and we didn't use the buildings. Even then I thought it was ridiculous. Why weren't we in those buildings instead of being out in those fields? And somehow or other our particular group found itself in an ambush. When you see the war, when you're a solider, the war is no bigger than from here to across the street. You don't see the big thing, the big view of things. We were trapped in a sort of ditch that we were walking through, and the Germans threw a lot of mortar fire, and a lot of us were killed. It was terrifying. And then getting out of there, I carried a guy – I didn't know who he was, he was one of us, and he had been wounded – and I carried him on my back and then I found out that he was dead, or that he had died while I was carrying him.

Then we saw dozens of dead bodies piled along the road. A terrible sight. We were on foot, we were marching on foot, and later we were in army trucks.

I wrote the two poems[1] then and sent them home in letters to my family. They were just poems of what you might call "circumstance". I couldn't concentrate and write music, and I wanted to do something to express myself in some way. I don't consider myself a poet, though. I haven't got the gift.

I was in a heavy weapons company, with heavy machine guns and heavy mortars. In an infantry company you have the light machine guns and the light mortars. And we were the "heavy" guys with the 30 caliber machine guns, these long things, with the tripod on your back and the canon on your shoulder. And some carried the tripods and some carried the canon. And others carried the ammunition. Our job was to back up an attack by the first line troops, the rifle companies. Our whole division was there. We were nevertheless under a global command of British and Canadians. Our platoon could be called upon to back up Company A or Company B or Company C. The heavy weapons company is Company H. And then heavy mortars might be called on to back up another company, and so on, depending on the situation. We were like small artillery for rifle companies, that's what the business of a heavy weapons company is. But I always thought it was amusing that as a musician I was a machine-gunner. And I just happened to be a machine gunner because the Army wiped out the language program! Otherwise, I would probably have been in military government or the occupation forces.

I remember in Brussels, on our way to the Belgian-Dutch border, in October '44, I was amazed at seeing a life-as-usual sort of situation. The city had not been damaged at all, and the people were really very friendly and very nice. They invited us to come to their place and to have a drink. I remember their hospitality.

An extraordinary experience happened to me in Holland. We were on the road going towards Breda. And further on we were going to the town of Etten. I haven't verified this, but I think it was the birthplace of Vincent Van Gogh. In any case, that was what I had in my mind at the time. As our battalion advanced towards the city, there were no Germans and no Dutch around. It was as if all the population had disappeared. And on the road leading into the city and on the fields around it we saw many chairs placed just about

(1) They appear at the end of "The Gunner and Messenger"

everywhere. It was really like a surrealist film, just with those chairs there. Then through the ranks it must have come back to us to be wary of the chairs because they represented mines, that the people in the city had put the chairs over the spots where the Germans had put all the mines. And I've always thought that would be an extraordinary scene in a film. In fact, all the people in the city were in their homes; they weren't outside. As we went through they greeted us with tears in their eyes, and they invited us to have a glass of fresh milk and things like that. I was very impressed by that whole experience.

And then they took us out of there. In Holland we would go in one direction, and then they would put us in trucks and take us somewhere else and then take us somewhere else again. I never could make any sense of what was happening. And I don't imagine there was very much sense. I think there was an awful lot of disorder. They took us out of there and put us in Aachen – or Aix-la-Chapelle – and there I think we relieved, as far as I remember, the lst Division. And from there we went all the way to the eastern part of Germany, to the end of the war, and met the Russians, not far from Leipzig.

Our letters were censored. The officers would occasionally read letters because we weren't supposed to say where we were. My lieutenant always read my letters. He thought I was some kind of a crazy person. I don't think he'd ever really seen anyone of any artistic bent, and the fact that I was sending poems back home – I mean, that was beyond him.

It began to be known that I had gone to college and could also speak German, so they made me a messenger. There were two of us – Kelly and Kurtz. The Captain had noticed that my lieutenant was sending me out more than Kelly and he wanted to find out why. I remember overhearing the conversation. The lieutenant saying, "Oh, well, I send out Kurtz because he can see the dead and dying and it doesn't faze him. He's an artist who doesn't even know what's happening. It makes no impression on him." And I felt like saying, "My God, what am I supposed to do? Cry? Have hysterics?" I had a job to do, and I did it. And that was all.

Another time, we were north of Bastogne, near the town of Düren. This was in Germany, but it was just over the Belgian-Dutch border. They sent me back because I had something many GI's had – a bad case of diarrhea. The medics just laughed. They said "put in a stopper" – GI language was like that – but they kept me there for a few days. I saw a captain I knew and he asked me what I was doing there. I explained, and he said, "You look pretty bad. Why don't you stay awhile?" And I said, "Well, I can't. I'm only here for three days." And he said, "Well, I'll see your captain." But the next day, or the day after, my captain came to the barracks in the rest area where I was lying on a cot. And he said, "Kurtz, get into the jeep. We're going back up front." Then he took me into his tent. There were electric lights and everything was dark. And he said, "What's your story because I'll have you court-martialed and shot if..." Even at the time I knew it was very difficult to get someone court-martialed and shot and that he was just scaring the hell out of me. And so I explained to him that I had seen Captain so-and-so and he told me that he would see you and that I was in a pretty bad way and all that sort of thing. And he said, "Well, I don't know any Captain so-and-so and, in any case, he didn't say anything to me. Go back to your platoon." I didn't hear anything more about it, except when pay-day came, I wasn't paid. That's against military law. You have to be court-martialed to have your pay docked. And he grandly told the whole company that I had been AWOL. And he said, "You know why you're not being paid this month." And I saluted very smartly and I said, "Yes, sir." Because I knew if I complained, he wouldn't court-martial me, but he would send me to a rifle company. And I was smart enough to know that, and so I didn't complain. I'm sure that he didn't put the money in his pocket. He was too honest for that. But he wanted to make an example out of me because of this incident.

When we were in Düren and even before in Normandy, during those waiting periods, they would take me out of my platoon and a bunch of us would put on army shows. I'd make up songs and we'd all write the words. Then I'd play them on the piano. We enjoyed doing it because it certainly changed the atmosphere for us! And so we'd work out a little scenario, Lord knows what, and try to think up some jokes and sketches. That kind of thing never happened when we were in action. It would be while we were waiting to go somewhere. We'd already done it at Camp Carson, too. The same group always worked together on the shows.

Another very vivid incident that happened was in the town of Frenz in Germany. We were just waiting to move across a very large field to back up Company A, B or C. And they sent out Company A across the field. The Germans were up above us on hills, surrounding the field, and they had it squared and quartered like a checker board and were lobbing in mortar shells in a regular sort of pattern. It was suicide. Finally Company A had to come back, and Lord knows how many were killed there, and then Company B was sent out and had to come back, and by the time they got around to Company C, I was certain that they would call off the whole thing because it was suicide. Our platoon was supposed to back up Company C and finally we got the order to move out.

I remember one of the sergeants – he was a very nice guy – had half a bottle of whisky on him. He called out to me, "You take half, and I'll take half. We need something in order to go out there." So I drank half, and he drank the rest. Then we threw the bottle away and we ran. Well, there were holes all over that field, and a lot of the guys were stopping in holes. I was not going to do that because I knew that the minute you stop in a hole you freeze up, and it's very hard to get out of a hole, to make yourself get out and run further, with all the mortar shells dropping around. So I just ran like hell, and I remember seeing one of the guys, who was just getting out of a hole...I remember seeing his head blown off by a mortar shell. There's something that happens to a human being when you're in situations like that. Happily enough, you deal with it, and you don't judge it in the same way than you do if you see it sitting in a chair or watching a film or you hear about it or whatever. But I did know I wanted to get over to the other end of that field. We knew it was somewhat of a haven once we arrived over there. And I remember finally getting over there. I would have been incapable of doing this in a combat situation. The field was about 200 yards long, and running over there, completely out of breath, I think I must have thrown up. A lot of the other guys had the same reaction. That's something I'll never forget. I'll never forget getting across that field. I don't know how I ever did get across it. I don't remember how many of our platoon got through, I think most of them did, but the bulk of the rifle company got killed. And during the night it was impossible for the medics to go out and tend to the guys who had been wounded.

They were all moaning for help and for aid. And then the Germans left. They went further on.

There's a musical incident that happened when we crossed the Rhine. It was in the area of the Remagen bridge. We crossed over and the idea was to do a pincer maneuver to encircle but not to engage combat, to get as far as we could and to meet the rest of our troops at a certain point. Then there would be other groups of soldiers that would clean up that area. We were in jeeps and in trucks, with mounted machine guns and tanks, tanks at the head of everything, and moving in convoy. It was a beautiful day, and that seemed such a complete paradox, with the war going on. And then word got back to us that our tanks were engaged, that they couldn't get through the town because of some German tanks. So there was a fight between tanks, American tanks and German tanks. We sat on a hill – it was like sitting in a stadium – and we could see what was happening below us. I could see the tanks firing at each other, and at the same time there was an American radio car playing "Death and Transfiguration" by Richard Strauss. It had probably picked up a local German radio station. I remember asking another soldier, "Do you know what we're listening to and what we're seeing?" Well, he didn't get the message, and I couldn't share it with anybody. We were actually seeing what we were hearing on the radio!

The thing I remember most about the war is the impression that you have of time passing. It could be only a month, but a month would seem like a year. After the invasion everyone more or less expected that the minute we managed to put foot on the continent there would just be a steady drive, which wasn't the case at all. I remember waiting around in Aachen. And of course there was the big wait in the winter of 1944 during the Bastogne disaster, with the von Rundstedt breakthrough. We were just sitting somewhere north of there. The Americans were very, very spread-out, because most of our troops were down trying to defend the American lines, which had been temporarily demolished by the Germans. But we were there, above all that, just waiting.

In fact the only nightmares that I had about the war were not about the dead and dying, they were just about the everyday waiting. The feeling that this is the way life is. It will never stop, it will always be this way. And this is all there is. Life is made up of marching, mud, combat, rain, and snow. And that's what life is all about. That was the impression I had during all that period of time.

Our battalion was the one that liberated the concentration camp at Nordhausen. That was a terrible and a very moving experience. Everything they say about those places is absolutely true. I saw it with my own eyes.

We went all the way to the eastern part of Germany to the end of the war. When the 104th went back to the States just after the war in Germany – they were supposed to go to Japan, but finally they didn't – I requested to do something where I could use my German. I thought I could be more useful than being a messenger in a heavy weapons company. And so I was attached to, I don't remember what the division was, but eventually I ended up in C.I.C., counterintelligence, which is a cloak and dagger sort of name for something at the time that was simply the arresting of war criminals. I was in that until January 1946.

That was the time I realized there was a great lack of soldiers who could speak German. I even witnessed the fact that in many small towns it would sometimes be the local Nazi party leader who was used as an interpreter. And that's why we lost face a great deal – you won't find too much of that in history books. I hope it didn't happen everywhere, but I saw it, and the townspeople, of course, thought it was rather odd, to say the least, that the Americans were using those guys as interpreters. The idea certainly wasn't to *use* the local Nazis. All a captain wants to do, of course, is to find someone who can speak the language. And he couldn't care less about the politics of the guy. That isn't his business. He wants to communicate something. And that's where military government comes in, and you realize that there are other things than just giving orders and communicating things. There is an attitude that one should have in regard to the population you're dealing with. The army needed interpreters, and they just used anyone who could speak the language. Let's say they weren't always Nazis, but some of them were.

There is an event at the time that made a great impression on me. It was on a personal level because on my father's side I'm of German origin. It goes back, my father always said, before 1740. We were part of what is referred to as "Pennsylvania Dutch", Dutch being a corruption of *Deutsch*. We had lists and lists of men to arrest. If we'd really done that, we'd have put practically the whole country behind bars. I was still a P.F.C., which was absolutely ridiculous doing a job like that.

Anyway, I remember interrogating a certain Georg – the German spelling has no "e" – Kurtz. That really intrigued me because my father's middle name was George. I went to his home to pick him up, and when he opened the door, I looked at him, and he looked at me, because there was a startling resemblance. He was a member of the party, but in fact he was an artist, a painter, like my father, and he taught art in a university. And in order to do that you had to be a member of the party. I knew that he would be released immediately, and I told him so. But I also remarked to him, "Did you notice a resemblance?" And he said, "Yes, indeed." And I said, "My name is also Kurtz." His name was spelled with a "t", like mine. That's unusual in Germany. In fact, he told me there were only two or three families in Germany who spelled it with a "t". We could have been from the same family, going back to 1740!

They later made me a three-stripe sergeant. Before the Russians took over the eastern part of Germany, we were sent to various factories to ask the leading personnel if they wanted to come to our side because the Russians were coming and were going to occupy that part of the country. All of us in C.I.C. were warrant officers, with no insignia, but in actual fact, only one man in our group was an officer. A major or a colonel should have been doing that job, but none of them could speak German and there were so few of us! I realized that the language program at Fordham could have changed that entire situation.

The big job was to get all the Slavic peoples over to the eastern side – the Germans were supposed to stay wherever they were at the time – then to get all the French, Belgians, Italians, etc. over to our side, to let them through from the Russian zone. The Russians were on one side of the river and the Allies on the other. And so we would send back, from our area, all the Slavic peoples and then let the western Europeans come over to our side. But how to tell who was what? Because none of this was really organized. We organized sending back the Slavs, but those people trying to get back over, they could just be anybody. In particular, they could be Germans, and the Germans weren't supposed to get through.

They put me on a bridge – there must have been bridges like that all along the line there – and every day for about two weeks, not more, when people came up, I was supposed to identify them and let them through or not to let them through. On a particular day it would be for two or three nationalities, and on another day it would be for another two or three nationalities. I had to devise ways, because I could really only speak German. I could *listen* to other languages, but I could really only *speak* German. My French wasn't very good at the time, but I could recognize French, and I could recognize if anyone was speaking with a German accent. Most of the Germans tried to get through saying they were Dutch. I devised a way of finding out if someone was really Dutch. Because there's a place in Holland called *Scheveningen*, and only a Dutch man can pronounce it correctly. I can't say it properly, only a Dutch man can. So if he said he was Dutch, I'd tell him to pronounce the word, and if it was not right, well it was a German trying to pass himself off as a Dutch man. Another time, I remember a cart and a donkey driven by a little old lady, with pots and pans and various types of clothing all around. She was British. And I said, "Well, what on earth are you doing here?" She said, "Well, in 1939 I went to Dresden for a holiday." She'd got caught in the war, and she'd been there ever since.

Later on, I remember the ship going back to the States, in 1946, because there were about three times as many soldiers on the ship as there should have been. We were stacked up in bunks, and it was very crowded. It was very uncomfortable, too. I think it took us close to 20 days. I may be exaggerating, but it was at least 14 or 15. We went way south and then came back up. It was a little dinky sort of ship. I was in a bunk, there were at least four of them high, in the center of the ship where they had the mess hall. And of course with all those soldiers there, when breakfast finished, lunch began, when lunch finished, and so on. We would eat standing up. The tables were very narrow and fairly long. You had to hold on to your plate because otherwise, someone else's food would come down on you, and yours would go on someone else. There was a constant smell of food, and I was seasick for about four days, after smelling all that food. For years I couldn't eat boiled chicken...

After the war, Kurtz returned to the University of Rochester on the G.I. bill, obtaining a Bachelor's degree in music in 1947. In 1949 he obtained a Master's degree from the Eastman School of Music. He then attended the Ecole Normale de Musique in Paris for two years.

Although he says he never really made a conscious decision to stay in Paris, Kurtz has lived in the French capital ever since. After "playing piano for third rate music hall singers" in the 1950's, he went on to writing music for documentary films, all the while working on his "Symphony for Strings", his first published work. Since then, Kurtz's music has been performed throughout the world.

For many years, Kurtz returned to the United States for a year and taught. He was a guest professor at the University of Michigan, the Eastman School of Music, the University of Texas, the University of Illinois and the Hartt School of Music. He is the recipient of a National Endowment Grant and an award from the American Academy and Institute of Arts and Letters.

Kurtz appreciates having one foot on each side of the Atlantic. He enjoys being able to work in France, has many friends and enjoys good French food, but he feels very much American and says his musical roots are also very American.

The two poems Kurtz wrote for his family in 1944 after his first night of combat – his baptism of fire – have been set to music by Aubert Lemeland.

Two War Poems

I.

Spring will come, the sages say, and flowers

Will be seen

And birds will surely come to play

In meadows that are green.

But I shall never feel the charm of April
And her laughter:
My comrade died upon my arm
And winter lingered after.

II.

I saw the dead, and they were piled in heaps
Along the road,
Chalk-white faces 'mid a mass of clotted blood.
I saw the dust clouds gather on that agonizing mass:
Army trucks and lines of weary soldiers had to pass.
I saw a dead man's hand stretched out to all
Who passed in supplication.
Futile gesture! dead men's hands stretched out
In supplication.
And the autumn breeze, forgetting that the
Dead were not asleep
Was playing with the bits of tattered cloth
Upon the heap.

EUGENE KURTZ
Holland, 1944

The counterintelligence officer

Warren Trabant was born in 1916 in New York City. He worked as a picture editor with Black Star Publishing Company and as a reporter-writer for Fortune and Life Magazine before being drafted in 1943.

He chose the Air Force in order to get into photo intelligence. However, after a year in San Francisco with a 4th Air Force photo intelligence detachment, he was sent to an army intelligence school at Camp Ritchie, Maryland. Immediately after attending the school, he was shipped overseas.

My first trip to Europe was on what at that time was called a "baby flat top": a liberty ship with a runway built over the deck. Baby flat tops were used in convoys, the planes – mobile in mid ocean – working as observers and bombers against submarine attack. Actually, the one I was on was not operative. It was being used to transport fighter-bombers and some intelligence personnel to England.

My class from Camp Ritchie consisted of interrogators of Prisoners of War, counterintelligence agents, combat intelligence personnel and G2 intelligence personnel. The transfer from Ritchie to Fort Hamilton in Brooklyn, then to the boat docked on Staten Island, took about two weeks. Not bad by army standards, considering the TARFU – meaning "Things Are Really Fouled Up" – that existed then. Although we were all classified G2, we were a mixed batch of officers and enlisted men. Space aboard was at such a premium there was little difference in the accommodation of Enlisted and Officer categories. In any case, counterintelligence corpsmen, both officers and enlisted men, wore no rank – merely a "U.S." on each collar – and carried a passbook identifying the holder in about seven languages. Both ranks were also issued a shiny, silver badge much like a policeman's shield.

When we reached England after twelve days in convoy, we were dropped at Liverpool, where the planes were to be unloaded. We were left to cope more or less unaided. We phoned the Intelligence branch in London – a miraculous feat in itself – and were told to go to an assembly camp just outside of Birmingham. This turned out to be a dreary, fog-bound place, which if described as "depressing" would be a compliment. We were treated like infantry, which I guess we were, but life in the Air Force and intelligence camp had spoiled me. Fortunately, we were not there long, and during the stay, I had an opportunity to visit London. This was the period when "buzz bombs" were landing with utmost regularity day and night in and around the city. Many were badly aimed, as the British were publishing newspaper and radio news reports describing center-of-London hits, whereas they were actually landing in fields outside of London. So the Germans, who were monitoring news reports, would continue to aim away from London, thinking they had direct hits. While this deception helped, unfortunately it didn't prevent all city-center hits.

Suddenly one morning, without any warning, we were put aboard a train and sent to Portsmouth carrying all our gear. It took us nearly two days for the couple of hundred-mile journey, which gave us an idea of the priority we rated. In Portsmouth we were bundled aboard an LST Landing Ship Tank – which, after two nights and a day on the channel, dropped us on the beach at Le Havre. Another TARFU, as there were no facilities or anyone to give us an idea of where to go or what we should do. A call to Paris got us aboard a freight train heading for Metz. No one knew why Metz, and when we got there, no one could explain why we were there. After a day or so of patient waiting, we hitched a ride on an empty truck rolling on the "red ball highway", the truck route from the Atlantic ports to the fighting fronts. Ten-ton trucks roared along this makeshift highway day and night, so it was not hard to find a ride to the capital.

In Paris, we reported directly to C.I.C. headquarters at E.T.O. – European Theater of Operations – Headquarters. I requested a post with a tank division. I knew from Camp Ritchie that a Combat Command of a tank division was as close as C.I.C. could get to the fighting front. Three of us were sent to the 14th Armored Division attached to the 7th Army in Alsace, but we had to get ourselves there. Told that a train was leaving the Gare de l'Est that night at 8 o'clock, we got ourselves to the station on time. The train didn't leave for several hours, of course, and when it did get under way, it stopped frequently. We were told the 14th Division headquarters was near Nancy, nothing more specific. Because the train compartments were crowded, we left our duffel bags in the corridor and settled in as best we could in the cold, 2nd class compartment.

The train shuffled along all night. In the morning, it stopped some miles short of Nancy. We were told the engine was out of fuel and we were expected to help refuel. We roused ourselves and started to leave the train, when we realized our duffel bags had disappeared. A real tragedy after having toted them all these thousands of miles! Luckily, I carried my toilet articles and writing materials with me at all times in a musette bag. We went to work, scouring the villages and farms for wood, coal or whatever to get the train under way again. It finally chugged off and we reached Nancy at the end of the day. Little of Nancy was left. The train stopped where the station had been – there was no longer any trace of it.

The 14th Division headquarters was nowhere to be found near Nancy. However, we did find a helpful Colonel, who sent us, as if we were a message, in a courier jeep to the 14th Armored. After we were under way an hour or so, we discovered the driver had no idea where the division was. From then on, we would find a headquarters every hour or so and ask. Sometimes we got little more than a shrug, but we kept on heading east, toward the noise of cannon. The jeep rode on bombed-out roads, plowed fields and forest paths and crossed a dozen or more temporary bridges.

At one point, we were told we would find the headquarters in Sarreguemines, some distance from where we were. We passed through a forest and as the road was indistinct, the driver turned on his lights. It wasn't long before shells began landing uncomfortably close. We finally realized we were attracting the cannon fire and turned off our lights. A bit later, after passing through a bombed-out village, we came upon a giant Senegalese with a gun resembling a small cannon. One of my companions, a Czechoslovak who spoke some French, began to ask him for directions. I suddenly realized that his French sounded as if it carried a strong German accent. I was sure the Senegalese was about to blast that mini-cannon our way, but he just smiled and directed us to the French headquarters not far from where we were.

The French were very helpful. They took us to their situation map room and showed us how to find the 14th Division. Fortunately, it was not far, and within an hour, at 3 o'clock in the morning, we walked into Division headquarters. Naturally, we were totally unexpected and carne as a complete surprise to the C.I.C. major, who, in spite of the hour, was up and on duty.

The next morning my request for a combat command post was granted, and I was taken by jeep to the medieval, historical town of Wissembourg, almost directly on the French-German border and about ten miles from the Rhine, somewhat west of the frontier. Thus, the Siegfried line was situated directly in front of us. This was Combat Command B, 14th Armored Division, a part of the 7th U.S. Army.

The function of Counterintelligence was to protect troops from damage or harm that might be inflicted by civilians in the area. It was our job to find and arrest high-ranking Nazis and, as the SS was considered a political organization and not an army, we also automatically arrested colonels and ranks above on the charge of being potential war criminals.

After a few days, we moved from the relative comfort of the town of Wissembourg to a rural community directly on the Rhine river. We were shelled almost constantly as the Germans prepared to retreat deeper into Germany. They were using what shells they had before retreating.

Our work in that location took us very close to the front lines, an interesting experience for someone new in the fray.

After a week or so we packed up and drove in a column with other vehicles, tanks, recovery vehicles, half-tracks, personnel carriers and the general's trailer, with a Packard sedan hauled on a platform just behind. We proceeded north, along the banks of the Rhine to Worms, where we crossed the river on a pontoon bridge set up between two destroyed bridges.

We were now in Germany. The destruction was devastating. Driving in the pale moonlight without any headlights through an almost completely destroyed Darmstadt, we realized how truly destructive war can be. A few hours later, we reached Dieburg, where we stopped and set up a temporary residence. In those first days in Germany, it became apparent that most work in the country had been done by unpaid, more-or-less slave labor brought from the eastern countries, but including some Dutch, Belgians, Italians and French as well. They were mostly kept in camps – crude barracks surrounded by barbed wire and raised guard houses. The inmates of these camps had apparently been escorted under armed guard every day to their place of work and returned at night. These unfortunate souls became what we eventually described as "displaced persons", or DPs. There were literally millions of them and, along with the Prisoners of War, they created a grave responsibility for the Allies occupying Germany.

Among the DPs were some congenial types, some of whom we invited to join us. Our unit thus acquired two or three English-speaking interpreters, who proved to be a great help in our work. We also had two Frenchmen – one, a baker, who became our cook, and the other, a butcher, who found good things to eat. He would slaughter a lamb in the field in a matter of ten minutes, bringing the carcass, leaving the innards, head and feet neatly wrapped in the skin lying in the meadow.

He did an equally good job with a calf. We raided the smokehouses of farms for pork, and occasionally our foraging butcher would find quail, pheasant or other wild game. Once, he carne back carrying a wild boar on his shoulder. This was always served with the excellent wine we collected from châteaux and manors along the way. Sometimes there were candles on the table. Our meals were so good we attracted the officers from Combat Command headquarters, which was never very far from our place of residence.

We continued to move, always a bit faster, as Patton had taken over our division, and we were literally speeding across Germany. We passed just north of Munich as the war ended and settled into an area slightly northeast of Munich, not far from the Austrian and Czech borders.

On one of my first expeditions into the territory, I visited Munich, which was almost completely destroyed – so much so that for a brief moment I felt some sympathy for the Germans. That ceased very quickly when we continued a few miles west of the city and round the concentration camp of Dachau. It was indeed a shameful sight. We were shown the first crude murdering machine used by the Nazis. It consisted of a small, windowless chicken coop-like structure set on a cement foundation. It had a door and a small pipe projecting from the base. Prisoners were placed inside, and the exhaust of a truck would be connected by hose to the pipe. When the truck motor was run, carbon monoxide would fill the space inside the hut.

The "final solution" building was far more sophisticated and efficient. We found piles of hair, boxes of false teeth, stacks of eyeglasses – all having been shed in the "dressing room" before their owners were taken into the "shower". The "shower" was, in fact, an airtight chamber with an entrance on each of two sides and little glass windows, where SS guards could watch the agonizing death of women, children and infirm men. There was a large supply of white flakes in boxes marked Zyklon B, the gas used to kill. On the opposite side from the entrance to the shower room, an exit opened directly to the furnace room, where metal slabs on wheels and tracks were pushed through multi-entrances to the ovens. Piles of ashes, both indoors and behind the furnace room, testified to the number of people who must have been exterminated there.

Back at C.C.B. headquarters, we settled into a farm village called Mettenheim, which wasn't far from Muhldorf. Mettenheim had a small air field and a Luftwaffe barracks. It had been a test and training field for jet fighting planes. I'd never seen a jet plane before and could easily imagine the outcome of the war had the Nazis gotten these into mass production.

There was also an enormous chemical plant. It spread for miles in a wooded area and was carefully camouflaged or completely underground. It turned out to be one of the factories that had produced fuel for the buzz bombs. Many people had obviously been employed in this endeavor, most of them being prisoners in concentration compounds throughout the area. While inspecting these camps, I came upon a huge lime pit, where hundreds of dead prisoners had been thrown during the previous years.

One morning, shortly after our arrival, I went off to visit a camp near Mettenheim. As I approached, the camp prisoners were filing out into the yard. As if on an X-ray, the morning sunshine exposed every bone in their poor, emaciated bodies. A Polish doctor was there among them administering the few drugs he had left to relieve the pain of some of the inmates. He told me that most of these unfortunate people would die if they did not get medication and nutrition quickly.

There was a simple solution: I went to the hospital in Mühldorf. Using the ambulances available, I moved the patients from the hospital to the camp and the prisoners into the hospital. During the transfer, I round several SS "automatic arrests" disguised as patients. The camp doctor took over the hospital, and we rounded up others in the immediate area that were in need of medical attention.

Our main occupation during those first weeks after the end of the war was sorting the German POWs, which meant finding high-ranking Nazi civilians. Some were in uniform hiding among the POWs; others were in the civilian population. They were to be sent back to Division headquarters, where the Allied occupation authorities would again sift through them searching for war criminals.

Trabant returned to the United States and his job at Life magazine in the fall of 1945. In 1947 he was named editor of a German picture magazine published by the occupation authorities. He remained at this job in Munich for two years and then returned to the United States. After a short period with an Italian picture magazine in Milan, he moved to Washington to work with the Marshall Plan. In 1951, he was transferred to Paris and has been here ever since.

After the Marshall plan terminated, Trabant worked as a picture editor for NATO for several years before going into the film business. His first project in this field was collaborating with Jacques Tati on an English-language version of Mon Oncle. *He later produced television documentaries for NBC. Trabant presently writes for newspapers in the United States and is the author of a book about Paris.*

When asked why he and his California-born wife, Jean, remained in Paris all those years, Trabant replied that he prefers French television and food.

Today a widower, Trabant has three children, three grandchildren and a great-grandchild. All – except his youngest son, who has become a French citizen and lives in Marseilles – reside in the United States.

SOUTHERN FRANCE

The W.W.I veteran under arrest

Julius P. Winter was born in Chicago in September 1900. His mother was of Czech origin and his father of German. Orphaned when he was fourteen, he went to work early and lived on his own. In November 1917 he enlisted in the army. After training in Missouri and Florida, he was sent to France with the American Expeditionary Forces during World War I. On the troop ship coming over, seven non-commissioned officers died of Spanish flu. He says each of them went down to the ship hospital to visit a friend and never came back up!

Winter landed in Brest, went on to Tours and spent the rest of the war as a company clerk in Paris, working at times for General Pershing. In 1918, he was discharged out of Fort Dix, New Jersey. Returning to Paris to settle with his French wife, Marguerite, whom he had met during the war, he worked for the Office of Grave Registrations and later the Battle Monuments Commission. In 1928 he was offered a job at the newly-opened Paris office of Western Electric, a company with which he stayed for some 40 years. One of his first accomplishments at Western Electric was to install sound for French "talkies", for which he received a commendation.

When World War II broke out, I was a reserve officer living in Paris. I thought when you'd been in the army, you had to present yourself. So about five of us went down to the American Embassy to see the Military Attaché, thinking we should enlist. And do you know what he told us? He said: "We don't need you. We can only suggest that you go hide in the mountains until the war is over."

Well, I didn't go and hide in the mountains. I stayed on in Paris. I had a French wife, her mother and two children to support. I was there during the occupation. In the beginning, the Germans probably thought I was French. Even later, when they knew I was American, they couldn't arrest me because America wasn't in the war yet. But when Hitler declared war on the United States in December '41, I knew we would soon have to leave. I remember going to the office and saying good-bye to everyone, taking the *métro* home before the 5 o'clock curfew and packing a suitcase because I knew the Germans would be coming around to arrest me.

They came into our building at about three the next morning, but, that time, it wasn't me they were after. We heard them climbing the stairs, going up to the apartment above us and arresting the Jewish lawyer living there. By the time they came to get me a few days later, my mother-in-law could tell them I'd gone. Their reply was: "What a pity! He would've been very warm and comfortable in a camp."

Like me, my wife and daughter had American citizenship, so we decided to leave Paris. After hiding at some friends' for a few days, we managed to get on a train to Marseilles. My mother-in-law and son were French, so they stayed on in the apartment in Paris. My son, who was twenty, was a painter and a graduate of the Beaux-Arts. He joined the Underground and did everything he could to hurt the Germans . He didn't stay at the apartment all the time. He hid a lot, so as not to be taken off to Germany to do forced labor.

My daughter was thirteen then. In Marseilles, which was in the non-occupied zone, I took over the job I had in Paris with Western Electric. While we were living there, we crossed over the line of demarcation twice and came back to Paris. People fed us and helped us cross the line. Then the Germans invaded the south, too. I remember how sad it was when they took down the American flag from the Consulate and put up the Swiss flag.

There was a special diplomatic train leaving for Spain, but the American Consul refused to let us get on it because we weren't members of the diplomatic corps. He let a lot of non-American employees of the U.S. Consulate get on it, though. Anyway, we snuck onto the train, and the Consul saw us and wasn't very happy about that, but the train didn't stop before we got to Lourdes, so there wasn't anything he could do about it.

When the train stopped in Lourdes, the Germans arrested almost everyone, even the Consul. I think they were sent to Germany. We managed to get off the train and into town without being stopped. We were going to cross over into Spain by mule, but we had to get some false papers first. We had an address of a lady in Lourdes, and my wife and I waited while our daughter went to the lady's house. She lived behind the grotto, the place where all the pilgrims come. My daughter, who was very *débrouillarde,* got the identity papers and we met up at the post office. That's where the Germans arrested us. They must have been watching us. They took us to a small town near Toulouse called Villefranches-de-Rouergue and put us under house arrest, *résidence surveillée.* We lived there for three years.

Luckily we had money. I'd gone to the bank in Marseilles the morning I heard the Germans were crossing the line and invading the south and withdrew all my money. Without that, I don't know what we would've done because almost everything we bought was on the black market.

I remember an incident that happened while we were living in Villefranches-de-Rouergue. It happened on my birthday, September 17th, 1943. There were a lot of Yugoslavs who'd been forced into the German army stationed there. Several days before the 17th, they started a mutiny and killed some German soldiers. The *sous-préfet* informed Vichy, and Hitler was furious. Supposedly, he was ready to blow up the whole place. The *sous-préfet* convinced him it wasn't the French who were to blame, so the Germans sent down a Panzer division instead of bombing the town.

They arrived on my birthday. The guns killed all the Yugoslavs except for about 150. These 150 were stripped down to their trousers and lined up against a wall. Then they were executed by a firing squad. All of us, even my daughter, were forced to watch the executions. The Germans told us that could happen to us, too. The Yugoslavs were crying out to us for help, but we couldn't do anything. We had to watch. Then the Germans buried the bodies in a big hole. Some French people went afterwards to put flowers on the grave. They were photographed by the Germans and later arrested and executed for being friends of the enemy. After the war, we went back there and saw that the Yugoslavs had built a monument to those who'd been executed.

At one point, the Germans wanted to exchange me for some German prisoners, and another time they wanted to take me away to a camp. But, fortunately, nothing ever came of it. I think my wife and daughter went to see the *Préfet* at some point. Later on, I remember we hid two American parachutists one night, and the next day somebody got them to Toulouse. Then it was the liberation.

By the time we were able to get back up to Paris, it was October. The war wasn't over yet. My son was dead. He'd been arrested, then released. He had polio, but there was no medicine, no doctors. We got his body back, but we had no coffin, no way of informing people of his death, no way of getting him to the cemetery. We were fortunate, though. People we didn't know, French people, provided us with all these things. The church was packed, and it seemed many people knew of his death even though we had no way of getting the word out.

Following World War II, Winter went back to work for Western Electric, where he held various positions of responsibility in France, Algeria, Tunisia, Morocco, Italy and Switzerland. As General Manager for France, he was responsible for the laying of the first transatlantic telephone cable to continental Europe on September 22, 1959.

Winter joined the American Legion in 1920 and held many offices at Paris Post No. 1. As commander in 1948, he had the honor of decorating François Mitterand, then Minister of War Veterans, with the Gold Medal of the American Legion. Mr. Mitterrand returned the honor by naming him chevalier *of the Légion d'honneur.*

In 1959, after the laying of the transatlantic telephone cable, Winter was named officier *of the Légion d'honneur. He also received a number of other decorations.*

Director of the American Chamber of Commerce of Paris for many years, Winter was also member of the American Club of Paris, the society of the 40 and 8, the T.N.T. (Tell No Tales) Club and the Confrérie des Chevaliers du Taste-vin, a French association for connoisseurs of good food and fine wines.

After Marguerite's death in 1985, Winter lived with his daughter and son-in-law in Paris. As a veteran of World War I, he felt it was a bit unfair that, unlike veterans of other wars, he never received a military pension. Winter lived to the ripe old age of 97 and died in 1997. Towards the end, he said it was lonely because most of his contemporaries were no longer around. He is survived by his daughter and son-in-law, four grandchildren and six great-grandchildren.

PARIS

The widow

Born in Washington, D.C. in 1922 and raised in Bethesda, Maryland, Phyllis Mitchell married John Sullivan, an American pilot who had joined the Royal Canadian Air Force in 1941. When he was killed on duty in the spring of 1943, the 21-year-old widow decided to join the U.S. Women's Army Corps (WACs).

After basic training in Des Moines, Iowa, she was posted to Camp Upton Hospital, Long Island, New York. In May 1944 she was ordered to Fort Oglethorpe, Georgia, for overseas training.

It was very hot at Fort Oglethorpe and there were long waits in formation on the parade ground. We were waiting to be reviewed by a superior officer or for some other reason. As lowly non-coms, we weren't always informed. Sometimes, we'd look around and see groups of good looking blond men in olive drab fatigues watching us drill. They would interrupt their work digging holes or gardening and just stood there, leaning on their shovels. They turned out to be German POWs. What an easy war they had. We were told we were going to be in a very special outfit called the OSS, the Office of Strategic Services. But nothing more. We were able to make some phone calls home, and then we were sent up to New York by train and shipped out on the *Queen Elizabeth.*

The voyage took a record four and one-half days. The ship zig-zagged all the way across the Atlantic to avoid German submarines. There were 13,000 troops aboard on our crossing. They slept in all available space, in the lounges, dining rooms, corridors where space permitted, some of them on deck. The berths were in tiers of three and four, made of tubular steel with canvas stretched across that folded up during the day. The soldiers slept in eight hour shifts. Depending on their location within the ship, some of the berths were occupied constantly. The planning and organization required to provide food, sleeping quarters and allow for minimum hygiene must have been something tremendous. We were lodged in a first-class cabin with a full bathroom, with hot salt water, which was very sticky. There were about twenty-three of us in three-tiered berths just like those on the decks and in the large salons of the ship. We were not let out of that cabin very often. Once a day we were allowed on deck. MPs were posted at either end of the corridor.

Meals were served twice a day. Our assigned dining room was down below. There was no air-conditioning such as exists today; ventilation was very poor, especially on the lower decks, where it was extremely hot and muggy. I can remember seeing those poor soldiers, sleeping or resting on the floor of cabins, their heads extended out into the corridor, trying to get some air. We had to step over them to reach our mess, which was situated over the second class swimming pool. The trip down was so unpleasant and the smell so awful that after the first day we started taking turns, the stronger ones bringing back food for the queasy. It was practically our only chance of getting out of the cabin, though we did have a reserved deck area – a small space that had been used in happier times for passengers to walk their dogs – and could get up there once a day to breathe some fresh air.

What I remember most about the trip is a constant sense of movement. The ship was never still. There were lines of men walking along the corridors, going up and down the stairs. When we left our cabin area, we, too, were always in line, never alone, always escorted. Some of the men would wink, or smile, or say "hi", but since there was no stopping those lines, a conversation never came to pass.

We docked in Scotland and then took a train to Bradford, England, a holding area, and from there on to London, where we arrived on June 6th, 1944. We were billeted in a town house on Upper Brook Street, two blocks from Grosvenor Square. That night we had our first contact with the buzz bombs – also called V-1s and "doodle bugs" – which were actually missiles. There were no air raid sirens. There was never an 'All Clear' as those things came over all night and all day. First you would hear one coming closer and closer, then the engine would shut down and after that there was a short period of silence, followed by a great BOOM. It always seemed as if there were more of them at night.

About fifteen of us slept in a large reception room on the first floor. (a European first floor, an American second floor) The cots were arranged head-to-foot, foot-to-head, Army-style, so as to limit the transmission of germs, and colds. I was last on a line, next to a large window, and because of the head-to-foot arrangement, my head came out in front of the window, while my legs and feet were lined up next to the wall. When a V-1 came near, the window would rattle and shake. There were times when I felt certain our building was going to get it. It could be spooky. I slept with the upper part of my body protected by the wall and had to let my legs and feet take their chances! But because there were inspections, I was obliged to make my bed up regulation-fashion every morning. And believe it or not, the duty roster called for us, turn by turn, to scrub the marble steps that led to our sleeping quarters!

We'd often be awake all or part of the night because of the bombs coming over. Some of the women would get to talking in their bunks. There was a large contingent from Texas and other parts of the South. I remember Billy Wade from Big Sandy, Texas, (population 300), discussing the Civil War with a girl from North Carolina. There they were in London, with missiles dropping everywhere, at three in the morning, talking about how the South just missed winning the war. We were all pretty cool during those nights, listening to those V-1s, not sleeping much, but on time the next morning.

I was a corporal and worked as a secretary, a job that entailed a lot of filing. The office would receive British military intelligence reports on such things as how many V-1s came over in the middle of the previous night, had been brought down, landed in London, or elsewhere during any given 24-hour period. Those reports never gave the same figures as the morning newspapers. They were always higher.

The British were as stoic as they are portrayed in literature. Several times, employees came in to work very late. "Sorry, I'm late, dear," the women would said, "but we were bombed out last night." Hundreds of people spent the night on the subway platforms. They seemed to have their regular spots. Whole familes would bed down in the early evening while the trains kept running. There was a basement shelter in the building in our building, but I never went down. I was only twenty-one then and reckless, I suppose. I probably wouldn't have the same attitude now.

In November, several of us were posted to Paris. We were quartered with a group of Air Force women who occupied a hotel on the rue Caumartin, named the St. Petersburg. Our rooms were on the 6th floor. There was no elevator, of course, and no heat. One of our roommates bought a tea kettle at the nearby Printemps department store. We were able to have a cup of tea. It was very cold and snowed that winter of '44. Many of the women had chilblains. We had been issued two blankets, but when General Patton got to Bastogne, we had to give up one of them for his troops. The army went so fast that the supplies could not keep up. Not only blankets, but also food. We had a diet of spam and powdered eggs at our mess at the Royal Monceau hotel for three weeks or more. Literally, – there were cases of what was called 'trenchmouth' a first World War term. Things improved though, heat came on in the hotel and hot water. I can't remember very well, but there was no such thing as a daily bath, I'll tell you that.

Our office was on the Champs-Elysées, in the building that now houses the Biarritz movie theater. It was so cold in the mornings, we would stop off on our way to work and have a nip of cognac with a cup of coffee to warm up. The previous occupants of the offices had been the German administration TODT, that oversaw forced labor deportees. When a three ring binder was needed, we would empty their files, and put ours in. Actually, I believe that German women had occupied the Hotel St. Petersburg. All over town, French hotels and offices emptied out the German military occupants and put in the Americans. Whereas in London we could take a Sunday off to visit some of the parks and take bus rides, in Paris we were on duty seven days a week. Occasionally, though, I could get a free afternoon. Following instructions from folks back home, I'd go shopping for perfume. There wasn't much to be had. The bottles in the window displays were all labeled *factice*, "not for real." Rue du Bac was a good street for small shops. From there we would walk along the river. French civilians were on bicycles, motorcycles or in taxi-bicycles. These made up the only traffic you saw outside of military vehicules.

I would walk along the Quai d'Orsay, in front of the station, now the Musée d'Orsay. It was an arrival point for deportees from the war zone. They were transported by truck still dressed in the striped pants and shirts that had been issued in the camps. Once lifted to the sidewalk, some would go into the station, others would just walk off. It was pitiful to see.

GI's were all over town. They would come in from the front lines on 24-hour or 48-hour passes. They'd stop us on the streets. "Who are you, What are you doing here? Are you really WACs? Never seen any before. Just heard about." They'd say: "Please come have a coffee with me." They were really wonderful to us, treated us like queens.

I wasn't in Paris for the Liberation, but I was there for VE-Day, May 8th, 1945. It was a wild occasion. The Champs Elysées was jammed with people. Everybody was talking to everybody else, there was dancing in the streets, and drinking, always lots of drinking. Excesses. Relief that it was all over, at least on our side of the world.

After Paris, we went off to work in Wiesbaden, Germany, where the OSS had set itself up in the offices of a famous German winery. The GI's in the building next door gave a dance for us. There was a non-fraternization policy, so there were no German girls, just us. I remember we danced to those sad songs, like "I'll Be Seeing You." And we'd all sing along to "You're my Sunshine" or "I've Been Working on the Railroad". When they were in England after the war, the GI's used to sing a ditty they'd made up to the tune of "Lilly Merlene", "We're leaving London and going to the States. We're leaving Brussels sprouts and going back to steaks."

I returned to London for a short while. Then after a crossing on the *Queen Mary* in October 1945, I was discharged out of Fort Dix, New Jersey. There was no fanfare, no flags, no medals. We were all glad to leave the stupid regimentation. I went into Manhattan, bought some clothes, then caught a train home to my parents'. My intention was to pick up my studies and work towards finishing my degree, but there was no room for a woman veteran in the New York city area universities. Everywhere was the same answer: "Sorry, but we must save the places for the boys." It wouldn't happen today, thank goodness.

It took a while for things to settle down. There are many things I haven't spoken about. You come out of such an experience forever basically changed. It seemed at the time that there was a whole part of me that I would never really be able to share with friends and family. That is somewhat true even today.

A year after the war, while she was living in New York, Phyllis met Raoul Michaux, the Frenchman who became her husband soon afterwards. They moved to Paris in January 1947 and have been living here ever since.

In 1960, by then the mother of two, Phyllis began to learn about the complicated American laws governing the citizenship of her children, who were born in France. Setting out to meet other American women married to Frenchmen facing a similar situation, she placed an advertisement in the Herald Tribune *and received fifteen answers. This was the beginning of the Association of American Wives of Europeans (AAWE), an organization founded in 1961 with Michaux as its first president. Still going strong today, AAWE now boasts more than 600 members, including a certain number of non-American associate members and several men.*

Like many other Americans, Michaux believes that by getting together, Something Can Be Done. AAWE has been instrumental in changing the outdated laws governing the citizenship of American children born overseas. Through its various programs, it has helped Americans married to foreign citizens raise their children as bilingual, bi-cultural, dual-nationals and has also eased the adaptation of new arrivals to French life. Michaux was also instrumental in founding the Association of Americans Resident Overseas (AARO) in October 1973. This organization played a leading role in persuading the U.S. Congress to pass the Overseas Voters Rights Act of 1975. Since then, it has continued its action on behalf of overseas Americans, who now number more than five million, in the areas of citizens' rights, absentee voting, fair taxation, and health care.

Michaux worked for many years in the Information Service of the American Chamber of Commerce. Now retired, she is still active in the organizations she helped to found. She is the author of the book The Unknown Ambassadors, *published in 1996, which describes the work of AAWE and AARO, and is currently at work on her autobiography.*

Phyllis and Raoul Michaux have a son and a daughter and eight grandchildren, all living in France.

THOSE LEFT BEHIND

Omaha

Slumbering souls,
Mingled and broken
From the weight of arms set free Slumbering souls
Towards the depths of the sea, Forever.

So much rain
So much wind
So many waves afar
And so many seasons
Above you, Forever...

So many thoughts
So many tears
So much sorrow still today
So many gazes at your graves
And the same songs of sea-birds
Already yours for so long
Forever...

Destined for a golden wedding In the endless days of summer
    –Oh, the green paradise of your lost loves–
So far from the thick forest
Where the birds of Maine
And the flowers of Louisiana
No longer await you.
Sleep at last, Soldiers of June,
Army of an impossible return,
Slumbering souls,
Mingled and broken,
From the longest day to eternity.

AUBERT LEMELAND
(Translated by Hilary Kaiser)

AFTERWARD

Some of the veterans I interviewed, feeling the need to share their experiences with other Americans who lived through the war, joined a veterans' association. Several American veterans associations do, in fact, exist in France.

One of these is the American Legion. This national organisation was actually first conceived of in Paris after World War I by a group of American officers and enlisted men who had remained in France to handle U.S. withdrawal from Europe. With the support of General Pershing and Colonel Theodore Roosevelt, Jr., they organized several caucuses and adopted a constitution in the spring of 1919. The Paris post, whose charter dates back to December 1919, is Post No. One of the American Legion.

Another American veterans' association present in Paris is the Veterans of Foreign Wars, an organisation that was created in 1898. Benjamin Franklin Post No. 605 (France) was founded in 1921 and chartered in 1927. Also present in Paris are three other organisations the Reserve Officers' Association, the 40 and 8, and the American Overseas Memorial Day Association, Inc. The latter association, which is also open to non-veterans, was founded in 1920. Its principal activity is arranging and financing ceremonies on Memorial Day at U.S. military cemeteries in Europe. It also arranges for the placing of American flags on the graves of all American veterans buried in European cemeteries. U.S. military cemeteries are maintained by a governmental organisation, the American Battle Monuments Commission, which has its European headquarters in Garches, just outside Paris.

The veterans I interviewed who have not joined a veterans' association often told me they knew very few other veterans and rarely had the occasion to speak about their war experiences. It was as if the war was a part of their lives they had put behind them. Indeed, several people admitted that between my initial telephone call and our interview they had dug up old photographs and documents or spent an hour or two in quiet reflection in order to recall the anecdotes and stories they later recounted.

Whether they were used to talking about the war or not, I had the impression that all of the people I interviewed found the experience of sharing their memories a worthwhile one. They were often surprised at how recollections would come back as they spoke. They also enjoyed seeing their remembrances in print. What better reward for a writer than to hear one veteran exclaim, as he finished reading his account : "I'm certainly looking forward to showing this to my grandchildren. Now they'll know what their grandfather did during the war."

LIST OF INTERVIEWEES

Achevé d'imprimer en avril 2004
sur les Presses de Ferre Olsina S.A.
Barcelone, Espagne
pour le compte des Éditions Heimdal